About this book:

The Character of Our Discontent grew out of the author's conviction that pastors do not preach enough about the Old Testament. The result is 19 chapters, each of which represents a sermon on an Old Testament character. These sermons are lively, fast paced, and practical yet are rooted in sound scholarship and are examples of the homiletical art.

Christians who would like to learn how the Old Testament can enlighten and guide their Christian walk and pastors who would like to learn how to preach more effectively from the Old Testament will both find these sermons an invaluable aid.

While Dr. Bevere specializes in the New Testament and theology, he believes that pastors (and academics as well) can preach and teach effectively outside their areas of specialty. Indeed, they must, and this teaching can enrich their own learning and the fields of study into which they venture.

The Character of Our Discontent is an adventure in preaching and it invites us into the adventure of living in relationship with God, an adventure that has similar characteristics whether we are learning about God's call to Abraham or how a call to mission in Africa came to a contemporary English teacher nearing retirement.

Allan R. Bevere is the pastor of First United Methodist Church in Cambridge, Ohio and a Professional Fellow in Theology at Ashland Theological Seminary in Ashland, Ohio. He received his Ph.D from the University of Durham, U.K. He has written two books, *Sharing in the Inheritance: Identity and the Moral Life in Colossians* and *All Is Not As It Seems: Random Reflections on Faith, Ethics, and Politics*, and is currently working on several more. He has published sermons, contributed articles to a Bible Dictionary, and most recently contributed a chapter to *Jesus and Paul: Global Perspectives in Honor of James D. G. Dunn for His 70th Birthday*. Bevere engages in a teaching mission in Cuba with the United Methodist Church. He is married and has four children.

THE CHARACTER OF OUR DISCONTENT: OLD TESTAMENT PORTRAITS FOR CONTEMPORARY TIMES

Allan R. Bevere

Energion Publications

P. O. Box 841

Gonzalez, FL 32560

www.energionpubs.com

Energion Publications

P. O. Box 841

Gonzalez, FL 32560

Cover Design: Nick May

ISBN10: 1-893729-78-8
ISBN13: 978-1-893729-78-0
Library of Congress Control Number: 2010927960

To my wife, Carol—

constant and loving companion,

faithful follower of Jesus.

Contents

Preface

The chapters of this book were first spoken. They were sermons written from two convictions. The first is that the Old Testament is relevant and authoritative in the same way as the New Testament. While most Christians would acknowledge the truth of that claim, for all practical purposes, the Old Testament is often treated as an appendix to the New Testament, even though it comes first. It must not be forgotten that what Christians call the Old Testament were the Scriptures of Jesus and Paul. They drank deeply from the well of its wisdom. They quoted from it. Jesus embraced it and utilized its narratives in word and in symbolic deed to display the nature of his ministry on behalf of Israel. Paul too saw the story of Jesus in its pages, and was the first major Christian thinker to reflect on its implications. Without the Old Testament, there would be no New Testament. Like our Lord and that great Apostle to the Gentiles, we too must drink deeply from that same well of wisdom.

The second conviction that gave birth to these sermons is that pastors do not preach enough from the Old Testament, myself included. In looking back over the Scriptures I had chosen to preach on over a period of a few years, I was frankly embarrassed at how little I had worked in the texts of the Old Testament. These sermons were an attempt to remedy that situation.

Being a full time pastor and an adjunct professor, I live in two worlds. The former is the world of generalization in many areas of study. The latter is the world of specialization. My training is not in Old Testament, though as a pastor I preach from it and teach it. While I understand why specialization is important in academia, I also find it unfortunate that the scholarly community has become so overly specialized, that it is almost an unpardonable sin to think that someone trained in New Testament can write in the area of Old Testament studies, and those trained in Old Testament can trespass into the domain of constructive theology. And God forbid that a theologian might write a commentary! It is almost as if a scholar's formal training type casts her or him into a certain role with a particular script from which there can be no deviation. The advantage I have in being an adjunct professor is that I am not limited by such boundaries. My formal training is in theological ethics and New Testament with recent years being devoted more to constructive theology, philosophy, and the relationship between theology and science. I have had no formal training in Old Testament other than the basic courses I took in seminary, but as a pastor I have preached and taught the Old Testament to church folk for over twenty-five years, and I have also done a fair amount of reading on the subject. So, while I have no doubt that plenty of others could have written something superior to this work, especially those who have spent their lives in the world of the Hebrew Scriptures, I have no hesitation in wading into the world of Old Testament homiletics. Indeed, in preparing and writing these sermons I found much enjoyment. That's really the only justification I needed for writing this book.

Acknowledgments

Sermons need an audience. I would like to thank the good folks of First United Methodist Church in Cambridge, Ohio for listening attentively to my sermons each and every week. It is a privilege to be their pastor and I am grateful for their faithfulness as God's people.

I would also like to thank a colleague of mine at Ashland Theological Seminary, Dr. L. Daniel Hawk, who teaches Old Testament and Hebrew. I did not consult with Dan directly on this manuscript, but it has been quite a pleasure "picking his brain" on matters that pertain to, as he likes to say it, "The First Testament." With some fear and trepidation, I look forward to his critique of my Old Testament exegesis. I also very much appreciate his friendship over the years.

Finally, I want to express my great appreciation to Henry Neufeld and Energion Publications for such hard work in seeing this volume through the process of publishing and distribution. It has become quite a pleasure to work with them as an author. I see my writing as a ministry, and so I am pleased to work with a publisher that sees its work as a ministry as well.

INTRODUCTION

"Now is the winter of our discontent made glorious summer by this son of York."

William Shakespeare

These well known words from *Richard The Third*, quoted often while ignoring the context of Shakespeare's drama,[1] is nevertheless an appropriate depiction of the human struggle to live faithful lives and lives of character in the midst of challenging times. John Steinbeck in his novel, *The Winter of Our Discontent*, deals with the struggle of living morally, especially when such behavior works against one's fortunes. Human beings are indeed discontented people.

But a word that better describes our discontent is not "winter" but "character." If we human beings are honest, we will admit that often our dissatisfaction in life is a matter of who we are. As that great Christian thinker and author C. S. Lewis rightly notes, the problem with people is not that they desire, but that they desire the wrong things. The Apostle Paul may have found that he was content in every situation (Philippians 4:10-13), but few other individuals can honestly say the same. Christians know all too well that while St. Augustine's dictum that our hearts are restless until they find rest in God, is true, even in the midst of finding rest in relationship with the divine, there is still plenty of discon-

---

1 In context of Richard The Third, the quote is one which states that the winter of discontent is over. Most of the time the "now" is interpreted to mean the exact opposite—that Richard, the character uttering the words, is complaining about their want, when he is celebrating a reversal of fortunes and better days.

tent as believers journey toward perfection. We are discontented because we lack, and often we are not sure what we lack nor where to find what we truly need. Indeed, too often what we think we need is not what we truly need. Character is not something Christians receive instantaneously at conversion; it takes a lifetime of forming and shaping as God works to restore his image in us. We may be in the image of God, but that image is cracked. Jesus wants his followers to become what they are, but the becoming is not easy.

The sermons in this book attempt to get at the character of human discontent. The biblical characters often found themselves dissatisfied. Sometimes they struggled with the call of God wishing it would go away. At other times, the call itself was not the problem; how to be faithful to it was the issue. But in the midst of the all too human struggle with the discontented nature of their existence, the subjects of concern in these sermons speak to the same journey faithful disciples travel at the dawn of the twenty-first century. If we look closely at these Old Testament portraits in the following pages, we will be able to see ourselves in their lives as well.

The Bible knows us because, as Augustine also said, God knows us better than we know ourselves.

1
Go West, Old Man
(GENESIS 12:1-9)

Periodically Carol and I have a discussion about retirement. While it is still twenty years away for us, it is certainly appropriate to plan for it now financially and personally. During our twenty-five years of marriage both of us have been wanderers given my profession, so we really are not attached to one particular geographical place, so we ponder where we might like to retire, and how those plans might change considering where our children, and hopefully by that time, our grandchildren will be living. We are planning for retirement knowing that plans do not always go as anticipated. It is important to plan for the future, but we must never forget that the Bible reminds us time and time again that God has a habit of messing up our plans, even plans for retirement. Such is the case in Genesis chapter twelve.

Abraham is enjoying retirement. Of course, retirement as we know it is a modern phenomenon; but still, at seventy-five years of age, Abraham was enjoying the fruits of many years of labor. He was also quite wealthy (Genesis 13:1) and he was living out his later years in the land of his birth. Is it possible for us to imagine how unsettling it must have been to be told to go west to an unknown land while living in retirement in the land of one's birth, and having no personal need to settle anywhere else?

Every individual called by God in the Bible is not expecting to be called, and neither is he or she anticipating where God will lead and what will need to be done. The call is always a surprise, whether it is Abraham going to a strange land, or a young man named Saul hiding in order not to be anointed king of Israel, or whether it is another man named Saul centuries later being told on the Damascus Road that he is about to become part of the very people he is persecuting. The call of God is never anticipated.

How difficult this is for us to embrace. If we are honest with ourselves, we will admit that we like life to be predictable. We enjoy the routine, and we do not want anything or anyone getting in the way of what we have planned. When the call of God comes into our lives, we discover that the world is not fixed, that at a moment's notice life takes a turn in a different direction.

Of course, not all surprises in life are good. I remember many years ago speaking with a woman in her seventies. She told me how she and her husband had planned for retirement, and how much they loved to travel. After his working days were behind him, they would go to places they had always wanted to see, but had never been. Then just a few months before his last day on the job, he died unexpectedly. She never traveled again after his death.

While Abraham's call was no doubt a surprise, it was a call in which God would bless him and his descendants. There would be difficulties to be sure, but in the grand scheme of God's plan, Abraham would be able to look back on his summons and know that it was a good thing he left his home to travel to the place where God would lead. The call of God reveals that there are indeed wonderful divine possibilities in a world where it is thought to be impossible. Such possibilities offer hope, not only for the one called, but for all those who will be touched by that call.

The call of God is never for the individual's sake alone. Abraham's children and grandchildren and great-grandchildren, and so on through the generations all the way through the centuries, would be blessed because of Abraham's obedience in going west. We must never forget that God always has more in mind than just us.

- God calls Abraham to be the Father of a great nation.
- God calls Moses to lead the children of Israel out of slavery into the land he promised to Abraham.
- God calls the Judges to lead the people in righteousness.
- God calls King David to make God's people after his own heart.
- God calls the prophets to remind Israel of its calling.
- God calls the Apostle Paul to take the message of salvation to the Gentiles, something not previously done.
- God calls Jesus to save the world.

An essential part of Christian character is confident trust in God. The writer of Genesis twelve indicates that Abraham receives the call and responds in obedience. There is no evidence of a conversation between the two where Abraham attempts to get out of what he is now being told to do. He hears the call and answers it. Abraham steps out in faith, not knowing where this new journey will take him and what will actually happen along the way. Nevertheless, he has come to trust in the God who leads, and so he confidently sets out in faith from the land of his birth. This is why St. Paul can say to the Romans, "Abraham believed God and it was credited to him as righteousness" (Romans 4:3).

I am not suggesting that it is wrong to raise questions concerning what it is that God desires of us. Moses does this on the mountain as he stands in the presence of God in the burning bush. What I am saying is that spiritual maturity is revealed in our unwavering willingness to follow where God leads, even though we do not know where the journey will ultimately take us, even though we cannot see the end of the path we trod, and even though the details of the future are out of our grasp.

God may call some to travel to places unknown, but God will call others to the journey of faith right at home. The point is not where God will or will not lead; the issue is not what the particulars are of God's will for us. The matter is our obedience to the call no matter where it is or what it is or why it is. Yet, the call of God is not as much an order to obey, but a personal invitation from God to participate in the plans of God to transform, to remake the world.

In his novel *The Testament*, John Grisham writes of Rachel Lane, the daughter of a billionaire. The very wealthy man dies leaving an incredible inheritance to her, even though he did not know her as he fathered her out of wedlock, and was simply not involved in his daughter's life. In attempting to find her in order to inform her of her newly inherited wealth, the billionaire's attorney discovers that she is a missionary in the remote jungle villages of Brazil. In her calling as a missionary, Rachel has sacrificed a life of comfort and plenty. So the question that permeates throughout the book is whether or not she will turn her back on her calling when presented with the kind of wealth that will give her anything of a material nature she could ever want. She not only rejects the wealth offered her in order to remain in Brazil, but she does so without any seeming temptation to do otherwise, shocking the billionaire's attorney, who cannot imagine anyone refusing such a fortune.[1] She chooses to participate in the plans of God.

There are sacrifices to be made in answering the call of God, to be sure, but when one considers what is gained as a result of being faithful, what we give up cannot come close to what we receive in the way of blessings. God calls Abraham to

---

1   As told in John H. Walton, *Genesis. The NIV Application Commentary* (Grand Rapids: Zondervan, 2001), 405.

sacrifice, but in the process God plans to bless Abraham in ways he could not possibly imagine before his journey with God; and in so blessing Abraham, God has blessed us as Abraham's spiritual children.

In my college days, I actually witnessed someone receive a call like Abraham. There was an English professor at the college who was well liked by the students. His last year of teaching prior to retirement was my senior year. He and his wife had financially planned for retirement years before, and they had their travel plans worked out for the next few years; and, of course, there would be the visits to the homes of their children and grandchildren.

But God messed up their plans. In the middle of that year, just a few months before the end of spring semester, both the professor and his wife received a call from God to the mission field in Africa. They informed their very supportive children of the situation, and completely changed their plans to the plan God had in mind for them.

After I graduated from college and went off to seminary, I lost contact with them, but I can remember sitting in chapel listening to his story and silently praying to God that I would always be as willing to answer God's call, whatever it might be and wherever it might take me. On the eve of retirement, that faithful couple answered the call of God and were no doubt a blessing to the many people they served in Africa; and they also blessed a young college student, who was so inspired by their courage and their confident trust in the God who leads, that he put himself at the disposal of God's call as well.

PRAYER: Lord God, as you so call us, lead us; as you so lead us, guide us; as you so guide us, journey with us; as you so journey with us, bless us; as you so bless us, use us to bless others. Amen.

2
What it Means to Trust in God
(GENESIS 22:1-14)

Author Marshall Shelley writes in *Leadership* magazine:

> "Even as a child, I loved to read, and I quickly learned that I would most likely be confused during the opening chapters of a novel. New characters were introduced. Disparate, seemingly random events took place. Subplots were complicated and didn't seem to make any sense in relation to the main plot."[1]

Confusion and questions are often raised when we read or hear the story from our Old Testament lesson. Abraham is commanded by God to sacrifice his son, Isaac. And while God relents in the end, many wonder why God would even command such a thing. To ask a father to willingly kill his own son seems so out of character with the God we have come to know in the pages of the Bible.

It was way back in Genesis chapter twelve that God originally called Abraham in his old age, commanding him and his wife Sarah to head west to a land of God's choosing. In Abraham's obedience, God will make of him a great nation, even though he

---

1   Craig Larson, *750 Engaging Illustrations for Preachers, Teachers, and Writers* (Grand Rapids: Baker Books, 2008), 160. Most of the documented stories I tell are quoted word for word, but are not put in block quotes nor set off with quotation marks. The reason for this is my concern that the change in formatting might interrupt the flow of the read. But do note that I give credit where it is due and that the reader should assume that each documented story consists of quotation.

and Sarah are well past child-bearing years and have no children. God will fulfill that promise in the birth of their son Isaac. But it will be years in between God's call of Abraham and the birth of Isaac. In the meantime both Abraham and Sarah attempt to force the fulfillment of God's promise in several different ways, the most notable being Sarah giving her handmaiden Hagar to Abraham so that he might have a son with her. He will, and the child will be named Ishmael.

So while Abraham and Sarah have certainly shown their faithfulness, at times they have also demonstrated their faithlessness in dramatic ways. At times, Abraham does not trust God, but neither does God trust Abraham to be obedient when it counts. God's command to Abraham in chapter 22 is for the purpose of finding out if Abraham's faith can stand the difficult test.

As we listen to this story we shudder to think that anyone would dare sacrifice a child, but let us not forget that in our own world children's lives are being sacrificed slowly by a rampant sex slave trade. There are parents in other parts of the world who, even as we speak, are selling their young children into forced prostitution—so much for human progress.

Even though the command to sacrifice Isaac sounds difficult to our ears, it really did not for Abraham. Abraham lived in a world where child sacrifice was not unknown. Abraham had contact with people who practiced religions where children were sacrificed. The fact that the Old Testament condemns such a practice demonstrates that it was happening. There is no doubt that Abraham was greatly grieved at the thought of losing his son whom he loved, but the practice itself was not unknown to him.

Abraham's faith is anguished. Here we see that faith is serious business. Abraham not only has to trust God that God will fulfill his promise to make of Abraham a great nation, even though the one through whom the promise will be fulfilled

(Isaac) will be killed. As I mentioned earlier, Abraham and Sarah tried to take matters into their own hands and fulfill the promise themselves. They were too impatient to wait on God and perhaps didn't even believe God would keep his word at certain times in their lives. Now Abraham has to trust that God will keep his promise even without Isaac, and continue to have faith even in the midst of indescribable grief as he mourns the death of his son.

Just as Abraham is about to do what God commands, God speaks and tells him to relent, "But the angel of the LORD called to him from heaven, and said, 'Abraham, Abraham!' And he said, 'Here I am.' He said, 'Do not lay your hand on the boy or do anything to him; for now I know that you fear God, since you have not withheld your son, your only son, from me.' And Abraham looked up and saw a ram, caught in a thicket by its horns. Abraham went and took the ram and offered it up as a burnt-offering instead of his son. So Abraham called that place 'The LORD will provide'; as it is said to this day, 'On the mount of the LORD it shall be provided' (Genesis 22:11-14).

There is a kind of pop theology in certain churches which believes that if we have faith and are faithful, things will always go well in life. So when things go wrong, these folks wonder if God is punishing them or they don't understand why God is allowing them to go through their anguish. We come to believe that the "normal" life is the "ideal" life.[2] Perhaps we even come to believe that somehow we have a right to a life without risk, and life without disappointment. Perhaps that view is revealed in our societies' propensity toward frivolous lawsuits. Perhaps we feel if something unfortunate happens to us, someone else must always be to blame.

But nowhere does the Bible ever tell us that faith will always mean smooth sailing. In fact, the biblical writers warn us of the opposite. They remind us that happenings and events will come

---

2   Walton, *Genesis*, 517.

our way that will test our faith. The writer of Ecclesiastes reminds us that in life there is a time for everything. We may not want to mourn, but at some point we inevitably will. We may not want to die, but that too will come our way. We place our trust in God, not so we will avoid the tough times, but so we can get through the tough times. And we have to learn to trust God when, like Abraham, the moments of life make no sense. John Walton compares life and faith to a roller coaster:

> "We cannot expect stability and security to define 'normal' because we live in a fallen world. 'Normal' is not the smooth, gliding monorail; it is the roller coaster with life's ups and downs.... Unlike the monorail, which functions to take us somewhere, the roller coaster is designed with the ride in mind, not the destination."

> "Some people see the roller coaster as frightening; others call it exhilarating. What separates the two groups? The former, I suggest, not only fear the queasy stomach but experience anxiety that comes from feeling out of control and, above all, worry that the cars will not hold onto the tracks. In contrast, those who feel exhilarated welcome the thrill that comes from not being in control. If, however, they had sufficient reason to believe the car would fly off the tracks, that exhilaration would quickly be transformed to the fear of the first group."[3]

We like to think that we are in control of our lives, and of course we need to take responsibility for our lives and our futures. We should buy insurance, we should save for retirement, but there is so much that comes to us that is beyond our control. The depth of our faith is not revealed in how we shape our present, but in how we live in the present, as we respond in faith to those things that come our way, over which we have no control. Abraham had no control over his situation, but he responded in faith even as

---

3   Walton, *Genesis*, 517.

he struggled and anguished. We too must trust in God. Faith is easy when life is good; faith is deepened when the circumstances of life leave us in a shambles.

I began with a quote from Marshall Shelley:

> "Even as a child, I loved to read, and I quickly learned that I would most likely be confused during the opening chapters of a novel. New characters were introduced. Disparate, seemingly random events took place. Subplots were complicated and didn't seem to make any sense in relation to the main plot."

But what you do not know and I will now tell you is that Shelley wrote these words as he reflected on the deaths of two of his children. He writes further:

> "But I learned to keep reading. Why? Because you know that the author, if he or she is good, will weave them all together by the end of the book. Eventually, each element will be meaningful.
>
> At times, such faith has to be a conscious choice.
>
> Even when I can't explain why a chromosomal abnormality develops in my son, which prevents him from living on earth more than two minutes....
>
> Even when I can't fathom why our daughter has to endure two years of severe and profound retardation and continual seizures....
>
> I choose to trust that before the book closes, the Author will make things clear."[4]

When the tests of life come our way, God does not desire that we be miserable. Indeed, God hurts when we hurt. But

---

4   Larson, *750 Engaging Illustrations*, 160.

what God desires of us when life tests our faith is that when we are forced outside of our comfort zones, we will learn that we have to trust in God in all things and in all times and in all places.

God wants to be able to say to each and every one of us, "Now I know that you trust me."

PRAYER: O God, help us to trust in you with all our hearts and not rely on our own understanding. Walk with us on this journey of life and may we place our faith in you in all the times of life; through Jesus Christ our Lord. Amen.

3
Giving Birth to What Is Right
(GENESIS 25:19-34)

It was Abraham Lincoln who said, "Nearly all men can stand adversity, but if you want to test a man's character, give him power."

The story of Jacob and Esau is a test of character for both men who have power in different ways—Jacob who has momentary power over Esau's well-being with a pot of soup, and Esau who has fraternal power over Jacob in being the firstborn. The character of both men is tested, and both fail.

In order to understand our lesson from Genesis, it is important to note two things. First, Jacob and Esau were fraternal twins who were raised by their parents to be competitive. In most English translations of this passage we are told that Isaac loved Esau but Rebekah loved Jacob. The Hebrew word translated "love" is better interpreted as "favored." Surely Isaac and Rebekah loved both of their children, but each parent did play favorites, and sought out any possible way for their preferred child to gain favor over the other son. Jacob and Esau were raised in a home where they were taught not to be trusting and true brothers, but cunning and conniving competitors.

Jacob and Esau could not have been more different. They did not look alike and they did not share the same interests. Jacob was a homebody; Esau was adventurous. Jacob helped out with the chores at home; Esau was out hunting game and providing food for the family. Jacob was more like his mother; Esau was more like his father. Isaac and Rebekah each had their favorite son and they did not attempt to hide their preferences.

Second, in the ancient Near Eastern world in which our story is based, the birthright was given to every firstborn son. According to custom, all male children inherited an equal portion of their father's estate upon his death, except that the oldest son received a double-portion. So, after his earthly days, Isaac's wealth and property would be divided into thirds with Esau receiving two-thirds to Jacob's one-third. It must have angered Jacob, (who was encouraged to be so by his mother) that he would not inherit an equal portion of his father's estate, even though he shared his mother's womb with Esau, and simply had the misfortune of being born just seconds after his brother. This sets the context of our story.

Apparently Esau has been on an extended hunting trip without any luck. Jacob appears to be away from home as well, likely with one of his father's shepherding camps where the livestock grazed in fields that were rather far away from home. This explains why Jacob is doing the cooking. With Isaac's wealth of servants they would prepare the meals at home. So, when Esau says he is famished, he probably is. It may be that he has not had anything substantial to eat in several days, and the only food in the vicinity is what is available in the shepherding camp.

Jacob turns Esau's hunger to his advantage. He will indeed feed his twin brother, but only in exchange for his birthright. Reasoning (without much thought) that his inheritance will do him no good if he is dead, Esau trades it in exchange for lentil soup, no doubt an unsatisfying meal to a "meat and potatoes" man like Esau. In his haste, Esau gives the double-portion of his inheritance to his younger brother who will now receive two thirds of Isaac's wealth.

There is no doubt that both Jacob and Esau are deeply flawed characters; Jacob in utilizing his brother's famished condition in order to receive something that was not rightfully his, and Esau in his inability to appreciate and therefore squander what he had received by grace—his birthright. And while we could devote much discussion to Jacob's appalling behavior, we need to focus instead on Esau's terrible decision to trade and therefore despise his birthright.

Two important things need to be said about a birthright. First, one received a birthright, not on merit, but on grace. It was by virtue of the birth order that Esau was to receive a double-portion and nothing else. At the end of the day Esau could not state that he deserved it, nor could he claim it as an accomplishment.

Second, Esau's birthright was a reminder that he was not a lone individual whose destiny was to be determined only by him, but that he was born into something larger than himself—a family that contributed to his identity, that helped form his character, and that had expectations of him that he was obligated, by virtue of nothing other than his birth, to fulfill.

Esau had not taken sufficient stock of the fact that his status as first-born was to have been received as a very special gift, and that it was to be cherished in gratitude revealed in the way he lived, and in fulfilling the obligations that he had. In not doing so, he literally despised his birthright. His status as first-born meant nothing to him because he lacked a heart of thanksgiving.

In our culture we no longer give such official and special status to the first-born son, which is a good thing, but all of us have received a birthright in the form of blessings. We are privileged to have received the birthright of living in a free society and in one of the most prosperous countries in human history. We have received the birthright of family and friends, and we have received the all-important birthright of our faith and our community of faith. Have we received our birthright in gratitude? There is only one way to know. What are we doing with the blessings we have received? In graciously receiving the grace found in our blessings are we blessing others? Or have we despised our birthright with ingratitude and the selfish pursuit of the trivial.

One of the great and early Christian preachers and theologians, John Chrysostom, writes of what we can learn from Esau, "Let us learn the lesson never to neglect the gifts of God or forfeit important things for worthless trifles."[1] People who are grateful for the blessings they have received are people who understand what is important. I have come to believe that gratitude is the result of a centered and grounded life consisting of well-ordered priorities, and that ingratitude is the consequence of a wayward life that emphasizes the inconsequential.

As a pastor, I have officiated at funerals for over twenty-five years. When grown children stand up to pay tribute to their deceased parents, not one has ever said, "I sure wish my Dad had made more money." Or, "It would have been nice if Mom had spent less time with us." And when they eulogize the qualities of their now gone parent, they don't talk about the stock portfolio or the fact that the cars got washed weekly, or that the grass was always cut so nicely, or that the carpet was always vacuumed. Instead they highlight character—they speak of love and commitment, they talk of faith and faithfulness, they reflect upon values and the instructions they received for living. In other words, they speak of their birthright. They talk about what they have received in order to live a faithful life; they reflect upon what they now owe to others as a grateful response to what they have graciously received.

Esau received trouble and years of estrangement from his only brother for despising his birthright. John Walton, an Old Testament scholar asks in reference to this story: "What can we expect from God when we show ourselves unworthy of his blessings by despising the values that comprise our spiritual heritage?"[2]

We Christians, however, are not left only with the bad examples of Jacob and Esau. We have the perfect example of our Lord and Savior, who lived his life in gratitude to his Heavenly Father by reaching out to touch and change the lives of those around him, and who, in his greatest hour of need, thanked his

1   *Homilies on Genesis*, 50.7.
2   Walton, *Genesis*, 564.

Father for his continued presence and prayed, not for himself, but for his disciples.

One Christian author has written that the world needs individuals

— who cannot be bought;
— whose word is their bond;
— who put character above wealth;
— who possess opinions and a will;
— who are larger than their vocations;
— who do not hesitate to take chances;
— who will not lose their individuality in a crowd;
— who will be as honest in small things as in great things;
— who will make no compromise with wrong;
— whose ambitions are not confined to their own selfish desires;
— who will not say they do it "because everybody else does it";
— who are true to their friends through good report and evil report, in adversity as well as in prosperity;
— who do not believe that shrewdness, cunning, and hardheadedness are the best qualities for winning success;
— who are not ashamed or afraid to stand for the truth when it is unpopular;
— who can say "no" with emphasis, although all the rest of the world says "yes."[3]

It all comes down to this: If we are grateful for the blessings we have received, it will be revealed in our attitudes and actions. If we are not grateful for the blessings we have received, it will be revealed in our attitudes and actions.

---

3   Charles Swindoll, *Living Above the Level of Mediocrity* (Nashville: Thomas Nelson, 1989), 107-108.

We have a birthright. It is a blessing that God wants to use that he also might bless others. Let us not despise what we have received, but use it in our church, in our community, and in our world to give birth to what is right.

PRAYER: God who gives us our birthright, thank you for what we have received as a result of nothing other than your grace. Assist us in the midst of the hectic nature of the daily routine in remembering what we have received, that we might give to those around us, and that you would use us to give birth to what is right in this world. We ask this in the great and generous name of your Son, our Lord and Savior Jesus Christ. Amen.

4
How Not to Win Friends and Influence People
(GENESIS 37:1-11)

In 1936, Dale Carnegie published his bestselling book, *How to Win Friends and Influence People*. Since its publication those many years ago, the book, which is still in print, has sold 15 million copies globally. In the book, Carnegie says that the one thing necessary in dealing with people in a positive way is to give honest and sincere appreciation to others. Perhaps Joseph in our Old Testament lesson could have used an advance copy of Carnegie's book.

Joseph was one of Jacob's twelve sons. Joseph's other brothers would be the fathers of the twelve tribes of Israel, but Joseph was clearly favored by Jacob, and the other sons knew it and resented it. As a younger man Jacob knew what it felt like to have a brother favored by a father; for his father, Isaac, clearly favored Jacob's brother Esau. Now, one would have thought that Jacob would have learned not to make the same mistake with his sons, but Jacob picks up the ways of his father and clearly dotes upon his son Joseph at the expense of his other sons. Jacob made matters even worse in presenting to Joseph a long coat with long sleeves perhaps with an embroidered fringe (not a coat of many colors as has been incorrectly translated). This coat was not just a gift for a son; it conferred upon Joseph's status in the family. According to custom, the oldest brother was the head of the household upon the death of the father, and entitled to a double portion of the inheritance. In this gift, Jacob seems to be suggesting that Joseph, who is clearly not the oldest, will be the one given the status of the oldest. No wonder the writer tells us that Joseph's brothers hated him.

Of course, what is a young teenager going to do with this preferential treatment but lord it over his brothers. We are told that Joseph was a dreamer. In Joseph's world it was believed that dreams revealed the future. Joseph has two dreams of ruling over his family. In the first dream Joseph and his brothers represent sheaves of wheat being gathered in the field. All of a sudden Joseph's sheaf rises up while the sheaves of his brothers encircle his and bow down. In the second dream the sun (Joseph's father Jacob), the moon (his mother, Rachel) and eleven stars (his brothers) all bow down to him.

Now it isn't Joseph's fault that he has had these dreams concerning his future status. One cannot help what one dreams; of course, years later these dreams will indeed come true. But a little maturity on Joseph's part should have led him to keep the details of the dreams to himself so as not to pour gasoline on the smoldering hatred of his brothers. But he cannot wait to inform his siblings of his regal future and, of course, their coming subservient postures. Verse eleven ends, "His brothers were jealous of him."

A man was standing in a motor home dealership when a motor home was towed in for repairs. The front of the home was badly damaged. The man was curious as to how the motor home had gotten so mangled, so he walked over to the service department to ask. The manager explained that the owner of the motor home had been driving on the interstate and had set the cruise control and then went back to the kitchen to make himself a sandwich.[1]

There are many reasons for foolish behavior. In the case of Joseph's brothers, jealousy is the cause of their foolishness. They plot to kill Joseph, but brother Reuben convinces the others not to take his life. So they strip off Joseph's royal robe and throw him into a pit. While Reuben is away, the other ten sons of Jacob sell their brother into slavery to a caravan passing on its way to

---

1   Hodgin, *1002 Humorous Illustrations*, 14.

Egypt. Then they dip their brother's coat in goat's blood and take it to their father convincing Jacob that his beloved son Joseph has been mauled and eaten by a wild and hungry animal. Jacob mourns inconsolably for his son. The scene ends with a father's pain, his sons' evil and deception, and young and arrogant Joseph on his way as a slave to Egypt.

This family is dysfunctional to say the least. Jacob, a father of twelve but acting like a father only to one. Joseph's brothers almost committing fratricide and selling their brother off as a piece of property because they refused to deal with their father's rejection in a way that might bring healing. Then there is Joseph who surely doesn't deserve what he received, but could have diffused the festering situation with a little humility and self-deprecating humor.

We human beings so often fail to realize how seemingly little events can grow into huge problems. If you travel down south today to the Carolinas and elsewhere, as you drive down the highway you will see a leafy vine covering miles of trees along the side of the road. Kudzu is a plant native to Japan and southeastern China. It was introduced to the United States in 1876 at the Philadelphia Centennial Exposition. The planting of Kudzu was encouraged to hinder soil erosion and as a forage crop for grazing animals. A kudzu vine can grow up to a foot in one day, so its plentiful nature was assured for farmers raising and breeding animals.

What was unforeseen was that kudzu's quickly growing nature coupled with the perfect southern growing season of heat, humidity, and mild winters led to a plant that would soon get out of control. It is estimated that in the south kudzu is spreading at the rate of 150,000 acres a year with a 6 million dollar annual price tag to control the plant, which is only slowing down the growth not containing it. What was once hailed as a wonder plant has now been declared by the U.S. Department of Agriculture as a pest weed.

How often we do not realize how our actions will play out in the future. What if Jacob had tempered his feelings of partiality for his one son? What if Joseph had exercised more humility in the honor his father had bestowed upon him? What if his brothers had not let their jealousy master their decisions? Sometimes we human beings get so focused only on the moment, only on what we want at the moment, only what we think is true in the moment, that we act in the moment and later regret that we didn't take more time.

We Christians have no excuse for behaving in the ways of Jacob, Joseph, and Joseph's brothers. We have the example of our Lord and Savior Jesus Christ. Paul writes to the Philippians,

> *If then there is any encouragement in Christ, any consolation from love, any sharing in the Spirit, any compassion and sympathy, ²make my joy complete: be of the same mind, having the same love, being in full accord and of one mind. ³Do nothing from selfish ambition or conceit, but in humility regard others as better than yourselves. ⁴Let each of you look not to your own interests, but to the interests of others. ⁵Let the same mind be in you that was* in Christ Jesus, ⁶who,*
>
> > *though he was in the form of God,*
> > *did not regard equality with God*
> > *as something to be exploited,*
> > *⁷but emptied himself,*
> > *taking the form of a slave,*
> > *being born in human likeness.*
> > *And being found in human form,*
> > *⁸he humbled himself*
> > *and became obedient to the point of death—*
> > *even death on a cross (Philippians 2:1-8).*

Jesus encountered the favoritism of the Pharisees toward only the rich and powerful. It made him angry and he had harsh words for them, but he never retaliated. Jesus knew the jealousy people had toward the rich and the blessings of others. He told such persons to be content with what they had received, but he never lashed out at those who were green with envy. Jesus saw firsthand the attitudes and behavior of the arrogant and he insisted that humility was the virtue of the godly. Jesus embodied all that he taught and all that he did when he gave his life for those who showed favoritism, and to the envious, and to the arrogant, and for all the sins that we human beings embody. Jesus has offered his life in exchange for our sins, in exchange for all those things that bring division between God and one another.

In the summer of 1994, a Virginia state trooper, who was a member of the bomb squad, and his dog, Master Blaster, became local celebrities when they found bombs at malls in Hampton and Virginia Beach.

That bit of celebrity evidently went to the state trooper's head. A hidden camera later recorded him placing a bomb in a shed that he had been asked to search for explosives. He was arrested and later did plead guilty to planting explosives at two malls, a courthouse, and a stadium. He told investigators that he had not intended to hurt anyone. The bombs—a cardboard tube filled with explosives and pipes filled with gunpowder and nails—never exploded. He said he was simply trying to enhance his image.[2]

Perhaps that was Joseph's problem. He was trying to enhance his image with his brothers. He was so narrowly focused on his own glory that he never thought that his eventual exaltation might serve the greater purposes of God and the greater purposes of those around him. Perhaps each and every one of us finds that we have the same problem at times.

Joseph will come to see the bigger picture that was beyond himself. Perhaps we too can see that same larger picture and where we fit into God's plans and purposes.

---

2   Larson, *750 Engaging Illustrations*, 499.

PRAYER: Gracious God, we have dreams for ourselves and you have dreams for us. May our dreams be shaped and molded and perfected to fit with your dreams, that we might reflect in our lives the image of your divine Son, our Lord and Savior Jesus Christ. Amen.

5
Who? Me?
(EXODUS 3:1-15)

Two young Jewish boys started attending public school in a one-room school in a small town in the nineteenth century. Of course, 120 years ago, education was different and religion was a subject regularly raised. One day the teacher asked the class, "Who was the greatest man who ever lived?"

A girl raised her hand and said, "I think George Washington was the greatest man who ever lived because he is the father of the country."

The teacher replied, "Well, that's a good answer, but that is not the answer I am looking for."

Another young student raised his hand and said, "I think Abraham Lincoln was the greatest man who lived because he freed the slaves and helped end the Civil War."

"Well, that's another good answer, but that's not the one I was looking for."

Then one of the Jewish boys raised his hand and said, "I think Jesus Christ was the greatest man who ever lived."

The teacher's mouth dropped open in astonishment. "Yes!" she said. "That's the answer I was looking for." She then brought him up to the front of the classroom and gave him a lollipop.

Later, after school, the other Jewish boy approached the first Jewish kid as he was licking his lollipop. He asked, "Why did you say Jesus Christ?"

His friend responded, "I know it's Moses and you know it's Moses, but business is business."[1]

---

1   Hodgin, *1002 Humorous Illustrations*, 138-139.

Christians rightly believe that Jesus was the greatest man who ever lived, but Moses ranks up there as well, and our Scripture lesson from Exodus records the beginning of Moses' greatness.

Moses was raised in Egypt in Pharaoh's court, but by the time of Exodus chapter three he has been long gone from the most powerful kingdom on earth. He is now married and pasturing the flocks of his father-in-law, Jethro.

Moses takes the flock to a distant place to find suitable grazing pasture. As fate or Providence would have it, Moses ends up at Mount Horeb, which we know more familiarly as Mount Sinai. Later after God has led his people out of Egypt, Moses will return here to receive the Ten Commandments from the Lord, but at this moment he is on the mountain either pasturing sheep or looking for stray lambs.

Moses encounters a sight that would cause anyone to sit up and take notice. It is a burning bush, which might not have been much of a sight had it been dry and struck by lightning in a storm, but here is a bush that is burning with fire, but it is not being consumed by the fire. To make things even more surprising, as Moses takes a closer look, a voice comes to him from the bush, "Moses, Moses!"

Moses' response is really a kind of stunned, "Uh… yes?" One wonders if he could hardly utter a sound, the surprise of the situation being so surreal. It is God. Moses knows well what the Israelites are going through in Egypt as slaves of the mighty Pharaoh; Moses has been there and has witnessed for himself the misery of God's people. God knows as well and he is about to do something about it and Moses is about to find out that he has new employment. "The cry of the Israelites has now come to me; I have also seen how the Egyptians oppress them. So come, I will send you to Pharaoh to bring my people, the Israelites, out of Egypt."

Moses is stunned. His basic reply is, "Who? Me?" God is asking Moses to go head-to-head with the biggest and strongest bully on the geo-political block. Moses is woefully inadequate and he knows it. Pharaoh has the most powerful army in the world. Moses has no army. Pharaoh has wealth and resources at his disposal. Moses is just a poor shepherd living hand-to-mouth from the land. When he asks God, "Who am I that I should go to Pharaoh," he speaks the truth.

But notice that God does not take issue with Moses' lack of stature. He doesn't give to Moses anything from the power of positive thinking. He doesn't say, "Moses, c'mon, you can do it! I know you can! Have faith in yourself!" God may not give Moses a personal pep-talk, but he gives him something better—his presence. "I will be with you; and this shall be the sign for you that it is I who sent you: when you have brought the people out of Egypt, you shall worship God on this mountain." In and of himself Moses can do nothing against the mighty Pharaoh, but Moses will not deliver the people—God will.

Moses has another objection—what if the Israelites do not believe him? What if he enters into their camps announcing that he is the one that God has chosen to deliver them and they say, "Who is this guy? What a quack!" Isn't that what any sane person would say? We see this stuff all the time on TV. "Rub this cream on your head and it will magically grow hair!" "Take this pill and you will lose that gut of yours, guaranteed!" "Order our kit for only $19.95 and working part-time from your home you can make $10,000 a month!" What a sight for Moses, this man who once stood in Pharaoh's court and who now works as a common shepherd, to stand before slaves who have daily felt the power of the King of Egypt on their backs, and tell them to risk their futures on him.

Moses has one more objection. Moses is not eloquent. He is "slow of speech and tongue." In other words, Moses says to God, "I stutter." Is it possible to imagine the sheer fright that came over Moses as he thought about not only what a risk it was to stand before Pharaoh with the demand of freeing his slave-labor force, but then to be unable to get the words out of his mouth? Can we not understand Moses' fear?

But God has an answer for all of Moses' hesitations. Moses would much prefer that someone else do what God has in mind, but God has Moses in mind for the job. By the time one finishes reading this conversation between God and Moses, it is clear that Moses has not been asked to volunteer; he has been drafted. What else can he do? He must follow in faith, remembering that he is not up to the task before him, but that the God who goes with him is more than adequate for what must be accomplished.

At one time or another, each one of us has had a task before us we wish we could avoid. We respond, "Who? Me?" It happens in the workplace, it happens in family and community responsibilities, and it happens in the church. We all know the 80/20 rule. It is true in the church—80% of the work is done by 20% of the people; and 80% of the budget is given by 20% of the people. At times all of us have said or at least thought, "let someone else do it," but is that the posture for those who follow Jesus Christ who wanted his cup to pass from him in the Garden of Gethsemane and yet did what he had to do for our sake?

Writer Bruce Thielmann tells the true story of a church elder who showed what it means to answer the call, not letting someone else do it:

A terrible ice storm had hit Pittsburgh, making travel almost impossible. At the height of the storm, a church family called their pastor about an emergency. Their little boy had leukemia and he had taken a turn for the worst. The hospital said to bring the boy in, but they could not send an ambulance, and the family did not own a car.

The pastor's car was in the shop, so he called a church elder. The elder immediately got in his car and began the treacherous journey. The brakes in the car were nearly useless. It was so slick that he could not stop for stop signs or stop lights. He had three minor accidents on the way to the family's house.

When he reached their home, the parents brought their boy out to the car wrapped in a blanket. His mother got in the front seat and held her son, and the father got in the back. Ever so slowly they drove to the hospital.

They came to the bottom of a hill and as they managed to skid to a stop, he tried to decide whether he should try to make the grade on the other side, or whether he should go to the right and down the valley to the hospital. And as he was thinking about this, he chanced to look to the right and he saw the face of the little boy. The youngster's face was flush, and his eyes wide with fever and with fear. To comfort the child, he reached over and put his hand on his head. It was then that the little boy said to him, "Mister, are you Jesus?"[2]

In that moment the man could have truthfully said, "Yes." He was being Jesus for that family.

Moses wanted someone else to take the lead in going up against Pharaoh, but he did take the lead, and he is one of the greatest figures in the history of our faith. Jesus Christ wanted his cup of death to pass from him, but he went to the cross and he is now the center, the focus of our Christian faith.

Most of us will not be called to do the kind of history-changing things that God called Moses and Jesus to accomplish, but we can do what we must in our time and place.. When the call comes down it is easy to say, "Who? Me?" But as the followers of Jesus we must be ready to be Jesus for others.

PRAYER: Lord God, you may not appear to us in a burning bush, you may not come to us in a fiery pillar nor through some audible voice, but you come to us nonetheless. You find ways to call each and every one of us to small but important tasks and yes, to large and significant things. Give us strength not to turn away from your calling, to hope someone else will pick up the

---

2   Larson, *750 Engaging Illustrations*, 315-316.

slack. As Moses on the mountain and Jesus in the Garden answered your call, so may we answer your summons and take up the burden you give to us; through Jesus Christ our Lord. Amen.

6
What Does Love Require
(LEVITICUS 19:1-18)

An elderly man was taking his evening walk. He was enjoying the crisp night air and the sound of the wind blowing through the trees when, suddenly, he heard a little voice calling, "Help me! Help me!"

The man looked all around and saw no one, so he continued his walk. Again he heard the tiny little voice. "Help me! Help me!"

This time he looked down and saw a small frog. He gently lifted the frog and looked at it intently. The frog spoke: "I'm really a beautiful young princess. If you will kiss me, I will turn back into a princess and I will love you forever."

The man thought for a moment, placed the frog in the top pocket of his coat, and continued walking. The little frog looked up out of the pocket and asked, "Why don't you kiss me?"

The man responded, "Frankly, at this stage in my life, I would rather have a talking frog."[1]

We human beings are obsessed with love. We sing about it, we think about it, we look for it, often in all the wrong places, and we give it more attention than most anything else in life.

Our interest in love is understandable. Our God is a God of love. Our desire to love and be loved comes from the one who created us. The problem is so much of what gets touted as love in our culture is far less than the kind of love that God has in mind for us to receive, and also the kind of love that God requires of us.

---

1   Hodgin, *1002 Humorous Illustrations*, 42-43.

The Bible has much to say about love, both the Old and the New Testaments. Some have simplistically drawn a sharp line between the Old and the New Testaments in saying that the God of the Old Testament is a God of judgment and the God of the New Testament is a God of love. This is false. The Old Testament has plenty to say about love and the New Testament also speaks of judgment.

Our Old Testament passage (Leviticus 19:1-18) became a critical teaching on love and its requirements by the time of Jesus. Jesus quotes from Leviticus 19:18, "You shall love your neighbor as yourself." These verses and the surrounding sections of Leviticus have been referred to as "The Holiness Code." In these verses we are told in no uncertain terms that love does require a certain kind of behavior that we must display toward one another. The behavior is described as "holiness." Now holiness has gotten a bad rap over the years. Some people have come to think that in order to be holy one has to walk around with his or her nose stuck in the air looking down upon everyone else. That is not holiness—it is arrogance—and individuals who behave in this way think more highly of themselves than they ought to think. Anyone reading Leviticus will know that people walking around looking like they have been sucking on sour lemons is not what the writer had in mind in referring to being holy; for a requirement of holiness, we are told, is acting on behalf of the outcast, those who are on the margins of society, those whom everyone else despises.

For the Bible, holiness is taking on the character of God in how we treat those around us. Leviticus 19 begins, "You shall be holy, for I the LORD your God am holy." We are to behave as God behaves. Way back in Genesis 1:28 when God creates the first humans, he told them to "fill the earth and subdue it." The Hebrew word for "subdue" can be translated to "put your mark on the earth." In so doing, we human beings, created in the image of God, put God's stamp on this world as we put our mark upon it. What it means to be holy is to reflect the divine image to those around us.

This is important. There is no other ancient religion that viewed its deity or deities as an example for moral behavior. Indeed, the deities of other ancient religions behaved terribly. The task of those who practiced other ancient religions was to appease the deity so that he or she didn't get angry and bring wrath down upon the city. But the God of Israel was holy and God's people were to emulate his holiness. As the people loved in the ways of God, so they more and more took on God's character, and the more holy they became.

So just what does love require of us according to Leviticus? Love requires a concern for justice for all; it mandates protective behavior for those who are most vulnerable; it insists upon truth-telling and honorable dealings; it rejects slander and gossip; and it categorically denies revenge. Love requires much more as well. The love the Bible speaks of is not a feeling, but a way of life. For those who desire to pursue holiness, they must desire not to be like self-righteous snobs, but rather to be like God.

And character cannot be hidden. It is like a sponge saturated with water. Lay it on the table and then press on it with your hand. The water is forced out of the sponge and all over the table. People can tell what is on the inside of our lives when they see what comes out under pressure and even in the midst of the little inconveniences we face every day.

I said that love requires holiness, but the reverse is also true—holiness requires love. In his book, The Moral Intelligence of Children, Harvard professor and Pulitzer Prize-winning author Robert Coles, writes,

"Ralph Waldo Emerson once said, 'Character is higher than intellect.' Marian, a student of mine several years ago, much admired Emerson. She had arrived at Harvard from the Midwest and was trying to work her way through college by cleaning the rooms of her fellow students. Again and again she met classmates who had forgotten the meaning of please, of thank you, no matter their high SAT scores. They did not hesitate to be rude, even crude toward her. One day she was not so subtly propositioned by a young man she knew to be very bright. She quit her job, and was preparing to quit going to school. Full of anxiety and anger, she came to see me, 'I've been taking all these philosophy courses,' she said to me at one point, 'and we talk about what's true, what's important, what's good. Well, how do you teach people to be good?'"[2]

The Bible's answer to Marian's question is not education but conversion. People cannot be taught to be good; they must be changed from within. The light of true goodness dawns in the heart only when the light of God shines there.

Jesus knew that as well. Throughout our four Gospels, Jesus is constantly getting behind the law to the intent of the human heart. Jesus knew well that just going through the motions of obeying God's commands was not enough because, sooner or later, one would lose interest, for one's heart was not in it. That is why in the Sermon on the Mount, Jesus says that it is not enough to say, "Well, I haven't murdered anyone." The kind of resentment and inner rage we can feel toward a person means we are already in danger; it means our hearts remain unconverted. It is not enough to say, "Well, at least I have never stolen anything." The very desire to have what someone else has means we are already in danger; it means that our hearts remain unconverted.

But Jesus also says that the more we open ourselves to God's love and emulate God's character, the more we will find it easier to love those around us, the more we will find it easier to love persons we have not met, and even those individuals we know but frankly do not like.

---

2   Larson, *750 Engaging Illustrations*, 88.

As the Israelites in the Old Testament are commanded to be holy and to love like God, so we Christians in the New Testament are commanded to be holy and to love like Jesus Christ, who came in the image of God.

Love and holiness are not optional qualities for Christians. They are at the heart of what we are about as individual Christians and as a church. When we reflect the image of Jesus Christ to the world in our holy way of life and in our acts of love, we are fulfilling the command of God way back in Genesis when we are told to subdue the earth, to put our mark, our stamp upon it. Jesus says, "You are the light of the world; a city on a hill cannot be hidden" (Matthew 5:14). "You are the salt of the earth. If the salt has lost its flavor, how can it be made salty again" (Matthew 5:13)? In holiness and love we are to reflect the light of Jesus Christ so the world will see what God wants of the world. We are to provide life with meaning and purpose; we are to be the seasoning and flavor for a world content to just meander on day in and day out, without knowing the larger purpose God has in mind.

In holiness and love we, as Jesus also said, let our light so shine before others, so that they will see our good works, and give glory to our Father in heaven. We are to be holy, for the Lord our God is holy. We are to love, for God so loved the world that he sent his only Son so that all may have eternal life.

PRAYER: God, our Father, may we love you in all things and above all things. May we reach the joy which you have prepared for us in heaven. Nothing is good that is against your will, and all that is good comes from your hand. Place in our heart a desire to please you and fill our mind with thoughts of your love, so that we may grow in your wisdom and enjoy your peace. Amen.

7
God, My Old Friend
(DEUTERONOMY 34:1-12)

It was G.K. Chesterton who said, "The Bible tells us to love our neighbors, and also to love our enemies; probably because they are generally the same people."

A humorous and certainly exaggerated line to be sure, yet is it not true that even the best of friendships can have their ups and downs? Perhaps the best friendships by necessity will have their difficulties at times.

This is certainly the case with Moses and his relationship with God. From the moment Moses received his calling in front of the burning bush on the mountain, Moses and God would journey together through victories and defeats, in the midst of good times and difficult ones. They would work together in concert as Moses faithfully led God's people in obeying God's will, and at other times Moses would try God's patience while God, on more than a few occasions, would have Moses baffled and confused.

Moses begins his journey with God as a reluctant follower. He answers God's call to lead the people of Israel out of slavery in Egypt, out from under the oppressive hand of Pharaoh, the most powerful ruler in the world. There must have been much fear and trepidation in Moses, but he is faithful. Utilizing Moses' faithfulness, God leads the people out of Egypt, which leads to great victory in the crossing the Red Sea. Here Moses displays great courage and moral fortitude. It is perhaps one of his best moments in life.

And as Israel begins its wandering journey through the wilderness, making its way over many years to the Promised

Land of Canaan, Moses also journeys with God. And as time goes by, Moses and God develop a relationship that certainly remains as master and servant, but something more begins to develop. Could that something be called friendship?

The founder of Methodism, John Wesley, struggled for many years in his faith. He served God faithfully teaching and preaching, and even in his willingness to make the hazardous journey to America to engage in mission work. Indeed, he came to America in the hope that his nagging doubts and concerns would be relieved, that he would find the deep faith and close relationship with God that he longed for. He did indeed find that faith and trust in God after he returned to London from Georgia. Wesley wrote that at the moment of his conversion, in his relationship to God, he went from being a servant to a son. While God was to be obeyed, what it meant to be a Christian was much more than simply a matter of doing and not doing. To be in Christ was to be in relationship with the very God of the Universe. Perhaps what faith meant in this context was to be on a journey, not following behind a master, but in walking side-by-side with a friend.

As Moses nears the end of his life, he and the people of Israel finally reach the destination they have dreamed about during the hot wilderness days and the cold desolate nights. Canaan, the Promised Land, sits right over the Jordan River; and now Moses is told that he may see the land, but he may not enter. Is it possible to imagine the crushing feeling Moses must have had to have come all this way in distance and in time to be able to see the prize before him, only to have it snatched away at the last moment?

From my older childhood years through my mid-teens, I played organized baseball. I will never forget one spring in particular as I looked forward to another season ready to compete on the ball-diamond. It was the year that I tried out for the traveling all-star baseball team. On the first day of try-outs over two hundred of us showed up to compete for fifteen spots on the roster. After several practices and a couple of weeks, I found that with every roster cut, I was still in the running. I eventually made it to the last round; and when the final roster was posted, much to my surprise, I had made the traveling all-star team, and not only that, I was playing first-string! I was so excited, I could hardly contain myself! I practiced hard and waited impatiently for the first game.

Just a few days before the season, my father approached me with devastating news. We would be moving shortly to another town about a half hour away, which would make me ineligible to play on the team. I spent that summer at a new house in a strange neighborhood, not knowing anyone, and thinking every day about that traveling all-star team playing under the lights of various ball fields in different towns in northeast Ohio without me. It was very painful.

Can we imagine for a moment how Moses must have felt? Here he was on the threshold, ready to reach the goal that had become the purpose of his life because God had made it so, only to be told at the last minute that what he had longed for was not to be? The reasons for Moses exclusion from the Promised Land are not entirely clear, but there are a couple of hints given in previous chapters of Exodus. Perhaps Moses was being held responsible for the consistent disobedience of the people of Israel that he had led, somewhat like the ship's captain being held responsible for the behavior of the crew. Moreover, there were certain incidents throughout the wilderness years where Moses had undermined God's authority in his speech and behavior. Those who lead are always held more accountable, not because they have a different moral standard from everyone else, but because they are to model the standard for everyone else.

Whatever the reason, Moses is to die with the Promised Land in his sight, but not in his grasp. "Then the Lord said to him, 'This is the land I promised on oath to Abraham, Isaac and

Jacob when I said, 'I will give it to your descendants.' I have let you see it with your eyes, but you will not cross over into it" (Deuteronomy 34:4 NIV)."

It is quite a sobering thing to look back on one's life and wonder what could have been and what should have been done differently. Everyone's life ends with unfinished business. If Moses only knew what he knows now at the end of his days, what would he have done differently? Surely Moses sits upon Mount Nebo pondering and wondering how things might have transpired if hindsight had been foresight.

But perhaps to dwell on what Moses did not receive, is to miss the point, not only of this closing chapter of Deuteronomy, but of the purpose of life itself. We must not diminish the great disappointment found in this story, but we must also not lose sight of the larger point that comes to us as well: "Since then, no prophet has risen in Israel like Moses, whom the Lord knew face to face, who did all those miraculous signs and wonders the Lord sent him to do in Egypt—to Pharaoh and to all his officials and to his whole land. For no one has ever shown the mighty power or performed the awesome deeds that Moses did in the sight of all Israel" (Deuteronomy 34:12 NIV).

The true goal of Moses' life was not to step foot into the Promised Land; if that were the case, the only truly significant aspect of his life would have come at the end. Moses' true purpose was being fulfilled all along the journey of his life— in coming to know God more and more each day, Moses lived his life in such a way that the writer of Deuteronomy 34 could state that he knew God face to face.

At the end of his life Moses sits upon Mount Nebo and converses with God, not simply as a servant would in a humbling way in response only to his master's wishes, but as two old friends who have been through thick and thin together. Perhaps they speak of where they have been, perhaps they remind themselves of how it all began while Moses was searching for lost sheep on the mountain, or when they were in Egypt staring down Pharaoh, and then reminiscing about the many days along the journey, even the days when their relationship was strained.

And as they look back, perhaps Moses comes to understand that his inability to enter Canaan is not a failure of his life's purpose, but just one last frustration in the midst of a life filled with disappointments. It is a life also lived in great joy because it was faithfully lived in service and in obedience to his God, who Moses now knows is also an old friend. And what a fitting tribute to a life well lived that God, Moses' old friend, buries him and delivers his eulogy!

Just before his arrest and crucifixion Jesus says to his disciples in the Upper Room, "I no longer call you servants, because a servant does not know his master's business. Instead, I have called you friends, for everything that I learned from my Father I have made known to you" (John 15:15 NIV). Yes, we may be Christ's servants, but Jesus came to this earth so that by his death and resurrection we would be more than that; Jesus came that we would be sons and daughters of his Heavenly Father and his brothers and sisters… and his friends.

The fifth century bishop St. Augustine wrote quite extensively on friendship. It is Augustine who defined salvation itself as friendship with God. And such friendship cannot be had overnight, it cannot be achieved instantaneously. Like all friendship, it takes a lifetime to build, to nurture, and experience.

And the destination of our journey of discipleship, of following Jesus, cannot be reached without the journey. May our journey of faith take us to the end of our days, so that it will be said of each and every one of us that, like Moses, we knew the Lord face to face.

PRAYER: Lord Jesus, what a great privilege it is to have a great friend in you. We know that such friendship is impossible apart from knowing you as Lord and Savior. Give us strength for the journey, wisdom to guide us through our years, and courage to walk where you lead, that we may come to know you face to face. We ask this in your name, O Jesus, our Lord, Savior, our brother, and our friend. Amen.

8
You've Got to Serve Somebody
(JOSHUA 24:14-18)

The religion of voodoo, more properly called Vodun, has a strong influence on the island country of Haiti. In the religion of Voodoo, the spirits control everything and everything that happens means something. If you are a farmer and your harvest is bountiful, that means the spirits ("loas" as they are called) are pleased with you; if the next year the harvest is terrible, the spirits are angry.

This view of the world can make it very difficult for Christian missionaries to keep converts. The voodoo priestesses of each village wield incredible power over the people. When someone converts to Christianity, the priestess will often put a curse on the person; and if something terrible happens to that individual later on, the villagers will see it as proof that the spirits are angry at this person for becoming a Christian. The temptation for the new convert in such circumstances is to abandon their new faith and return to his or her former religious practices.

I experienced this situation first-hand over twenty-five years ago as a college student on a mission trip there. Our team was in a very primitive setting deep in the mountains near the Dominican Republic. There was a farmer in the village where we worked, who had been a recent convert to Christianity. The priestess of the village placed a curse on him and the following year his crop failed. It was unimportant that there were crop-failures in general in many places surrounding the village. He was told that his woes were due to the anger of the spirits. The temptation to return to his former faith was great. The only Christian missionary in the village, whose specialty was agriculture, worked with the man, praying with him, studying the Bible with him, and teaching him better farming techniques, and tried to encourage him to keep his newfound faith.

Throughout the various planting and harvest seasons, he remained true to his faith in spite of the ridicule he received from some villagers and members of his own family. Over time as this farmer utilized what he had learned from the missionary, his crops were more productive, his average yield increased. Soon other farmers in the area began to approach the missionary asking, not only for help in farming, but inquiring into what it meant to be a follower of Jesus. One villager commented that even the powerful spirits of voodoo had to answer to the God of the American missionary.

That story highlights the importance of the choice that Joshua lays before the people of Israel in our Old Testament lesson. Joshua wants to make it very clear that there can be no middle ground in reference to their allegiance. They will serve somebody and their choice must be clear. It is not a both/and decision; it is an either/or choice. "Choose this day whom you will serve, whether the gods your ancestors served in the region beyond the River or the gods of the Amorites in whose land you are living; but as for me and my household, we will serve the Lord" (Joshua 24:15).

The other gods Joshua refers to were very attractive to the people. Those gods, just as in Haitian voodoo, were perceived as controlling everything, from the weather to the harvest, from moments of joy to times of sorrow. When things were not going well, the temptation to return to those false deities and call on them for help was great indeed. Joshua knows this and he demands two actions from the people of Israel. First, they must enter into a proper relationship with God who has delivered them. That means among other things, that they must be obedient to the covenant that God gave to Moses and serve in integrity and faithfulness. Second, the people must rid themselves completely of rival deities that threaten God's lordship over their lives.[1]

That day, the people would indeed pledge to serve only the one true God, but down through the centuries, Israel's history would demonstrate the difficulty in keeping that promise. Even though God would send judges and prophets, the local deities of other faiths would prove too attractive for them. Instead of worshiping the one God over everything, they chose instead to follow this deity who controlled the sunshine and that god who determined the harvest. They rejected the ultimate for that which was second-rate. Joshua understood, just as that American missionary in Haiti understood, that each and every person has to make a choice. There is no sitting on the fence, there is no such thing as indecision.

There have always been those throughout history who have wanted to sit on the fence and remain neutral when it comes to religious matters. The ancient Romans had the Pantheon, where the statues of the gods and goddess from the peoples they conquered were displayed as one big happy heavenly family. The early Christians saw such endeavors as idolatrous. Either Jesus was Lord or he wasn't. It was not a both/and situation; it was either/or.

And so today, many want it both ways. They want a little bit of Christianity, but not too much. They seem afraid if they truly choose in the manner Joshua insists upon, it will mean a change in the life that they now enjoy. In a culture that tells us to keep our options open, the Bible comes to us and insists that of all the options "out there" vying for our total and complete allegiance, there is only one real choice among all the options.

---

1   Trent Butler, *Joshua: Word Biblical Commentary* (Waco: Word Books, 1983), 273.

God did not raise Jesus from the dead to be just one more
religious option among many. Religious neutrality is not possible.
Indecision is indeed a decision. In this life, we will serve somebody
or something or some cause; and the Bible tells us that if we do
not serve God, we human beings usually end up serving ourselves.

Jesus himself tells his disciples and the crowd that there is no
middle ground concerning the human response to him and his
ministry. At the end of the Gospel of John chapter six when Jesus
calls for such a stark and clear choice, we are told that many no
longer followed him (6:66). At that point Jesus did not indicate
any willingness to negotiate the terms of their allegiance. He was
not simply a good teacher for them to pick and choose whatever
teachings they may have liked. He was not only a miracle-worker
to assist them with their needs. He was the Lord who had come
to offer salvation in response for their total commitment.

C.S. Lewis summarizes this quite nicely in his book, *Mere
Christianity*:

I am trying here to prevent anyone saying the really foolish
thing that people often say about Him: "I'm ready to accept Jesus
as a great moral teacher, but I don't accept His claim to be God."
That is the one thing we must not say. A man who said the sort
of things Jesus said would not be a great moral teacher. He would
either be a lunatic— on a level with the man who says he is a
poached egg— or else he would be the Devil of Hell. You must
make your choice. Either this man was, and is, the Son of God:
or else a madman or something worse. You can shut Him up for
a fool, you can spit at Him and kill Him as a demon; or you can
fall at His feet and call Him Lord and God. But let us not come
with any patronizing nonsense about His being a great human
teacher. He has not left that open to us. He did not intend to.

It was not just any god who rescued Israel out of slavery in
Egypt. It was not just any god, who led them through the

wilderness. It was not just any god who brought the people to the Promised Land. It was the God of Abraham, Isaac, and Jacob. Joshua wants to remind the people of that fact. If they were going to prosper in that land, if they were going to be the light of God to the other nations of the world, then they needed to hold the standard of that God for all to see. If they failed to shine that light in word and in deed, then no one around them would come to consider believing as well.

To get back to the story I began with, as more and more Haitians in that village were assisted by the missionary and as he taught them about crop rotation and other methods to improve their harvest, many in that village became Christians. It was not so much because they believed that his God had more powerful magic then the spirits of their native voodoo (though that was surely part of it), but they came to see that his commitment to them was the result of his commitment to his God, Jesus Christ. The American missionary's influence in that village became so great that one day, the voodoo priestess of the village traveled across the street from her house to his, and began inquiring about his faith. When our team left that place to return home, she was not a Christian, but she was no longer antagonistic toward that faith that she believed was an intrusion. In fact, when we would walk down the road past her, she would greet us.

That was twenty-six years ago. I do not know if she ever became a Christian, but there was no doubt in my mind as I left that place, that she was in contact with people who had chosen to serve Jesus Christ and no one else. I left knowing that she was in good hands.

PRAYER: Lord Jesus, in a culture of so many attractive choices, help us to choose only you. In a world of options always before us, assist us in excluding any option that denies your lordship. In a time when fence-sitting is so popular, remind us that you stand only on one side of the gate.

Lord Jesus, may we follow to the places where you lead, may we walk the path you trod, may we travel wherever you call. Amen.

9
Trivializing the Gift
(JUDGES 16:4-22)

A young man called his mother and excitedly announced that he had just met the woman of his dreams.

His mother said, "Why don't you send her flowers and invite her to your apartment for a home-cooked meal?"

The day after the big date, his mother called to see how things had gone.

"Mom, the evening was a complete disaster," he replied. "It was horrible!"

"Why, didn't she come over?" his mother asked.

"Yeah, she came over. But she refused to cook!"

Sometimes Samson and Delilah are listed as one of history's great romances. Those who believe this to be the case have not read the story from Judges chapter 16. Samson is selfish and self-centered. He acts not on principle, but is controlled by his passions. Delilah is greedy, willing to betray the one she supposedly loves, knowing that Samson's captors will treat him inhumanely. This is not the kind of romance that any man or woman should desire.

In order to set the context of the story, it is important to note that Samson was separated at birth for the special purposes of God, as one who would help deliver the people of Israel from the Philistines, a warlike and ruthless people who settled along the coastline of the nation of Israel. In order to demonstrate his special favor with God, Samson's parents were commanded to take a Nazarite vow on his behalf. As a Nazarite,

Samson would abstain his entire life from drinking wine, he would strictly follow a kosher diet, he would not come into contact with anything dead, including animals (which meant he would not hunt, something that was the norm for men in that day), he would be celibate, and his hair was never to be cut.

As Samson grows into a young man, he proceeds to break every one of those vows, and he fails to take God's calling and the gift of his strength seriously with his incessant sense of humor and continual playing of practical jokes, even on his opponents. He is so busy "yukking it up" all the time, that he gets in the way of what God wants to do for the people of Israel through him.

And now Samson has developed yet another romance—this time with a woman named Delilah. Up to this point, Samson has broken every one of his vows as a Nazarite except for one; a razor has yet to touch his head. Samson's enemies conspire with Delilah, offering her what amounts to about 150 pounds of silver—which would essentially make her a millionaire—if she can discover the secret to Samson's great strength. The lure of wealth is too great, and Delilah sets about her work.

One wonders how Samson can be so gullible. Three times she asks him the secret of his great strength. And three times, even though Samson lies to her, she attempts to bind him doing as he says. One would think that Samson would have figured out what Delilah was up to after the first time when she bound him with bow strings. Perhaps Samson's own passion for Delilah blinds him to what is actually going on. Perhaps Samson knows but does not care because he thinks he is invincible.

In any case, we are told that Delilah nags Samson until he is "sick to death." He finally tells her the truth and she acts upon it. When Samson is awakened with his newly shaven head, he is unaware at first of what has been done to him. His last vow has been broken and tragically we read that the Lord had left him. His superhuman strength is gone. He is captured, his eyes are gouged out, a typical act performed on conquered enemies, and he is given the work of a slave because he is now a slave.

I remember when I was a boy learning about Samson in Sunday School. We learned of his great strength and how, in the end he was faithful to God, and God used him to bring down the pagan temple defeating his enemies. And, of course, what I learned was true. But the lives of God's people in the Bible are often complex, and while we must start with the Sunday School stories as children, at some point we must move beyond them.

Samson is one of the Bible's most tragic figures. When he is born, there is so much promise and opportunity that await him. Even before his birth the favor of God rests upon him. Samson is set apart by the Lord for his purposes. He has been chosen and he has been distinctly honored to have the task of being one of Israel's deliverers. And in order to complete the job he has been given, Samson is given the anointing of the Lord and he is given the gift of strength. What a bright future Samson has!

But Samson's life does not achieve the hope and promise that was anticipated. Samson lives his life as one who trivializes the gift he has received. He can think only of himself and what he wants. When that kind of selfishness is combined with a lack of discipline, Samson finds it easy to break every one of the Nazarite vows that was supposed to set him apart as God's chosen instrument. Indeed, it doesn't even appear that Samson feels any guilt. Instead, Samson's way of life reveals that, not only is he not different, but that he is even worse; he is like the Philistines, the enemies he has been chosen to oppose. Throughout his days, Samson is unable to take his calling seriously enough. In the end his pride and practical jokes will get the best of him, and at the end, the tragedy of his life will be no laughing matter. Samson was not only selfish; he was foolish.

An article entitled, "How to Be Miserable," written by an unknown author, states the following, "Think about yourself. Talk about yourself. Use "I" as often as possible. Mirror yourself continually in the opinion of others. Listen greedily to what people say about you. Expect to be appreciated. Be suspicious. Be jealous and envious. Be sensitive to slights. Never forgive a criticism. Trust nobody but yourself. Insist on consideration and respect. Demand agreement with your own views on everything. Sulk if people are not grateful to you for favors shown them. Never forget a service you have rendered. Shirk your duties if you can. Do as little as possible for others."[1]

Yes, God was able to use Samson in spite of himself, but God could not employ Samson in the way that God truly wanted. God wanted to completely expel the Philistines out of the land of Israel, but Samson was only able to begin the process. Every previous major Judge that was called reigned for forty years. Samson led for only twenty. God wanted more of Samson, but Samson was happy with much less. God gave Samson everything he needed; Samson used what he was given mostly for himself.

Our talents are God's gifts to us. What we do with those talents are our gifts to God. God wants to use each and every one of us for his honor. But it is not a foregone conclusion that God will be able to use us. To be sure, we are given the necessary gifts to complete the divine task in our lives, but we must be willing to use those gifts, not for our own ends, but the glory of God. The goal is not our own reward, but knowing that we please God.

Isaac Newton, who was hit in the head with the falling apple, discovered and introduced the laws of gravity in the 1600s, which revolutionized the study of astronomy. Few, however, are familiar with the fact that if it weren't for his scientific colleague, Edmund Halley, the world might never have heard of Newton. It was Halley who challenged Newton to think through his original theories. Halley even corrected Newton's mathematical errors and prepared geometrical figures to support his discoveries. Halley

---

1   http://www.sermonillustrations.com/a-z/s/self_centered.htm

coaxed the hesitant Newton to write his revolutionary work, *Mathematical Principles of Natural Philosophy*. Halley himself edited and supervised the publication, and actually financed its printing even though Newton was wealthier and easily could have afforded the printing costs.

Historians refer to Halley as one of the most selfless examples in the annals of science. Newton began almost immediately to reap the rewards of prominence, while Halley received little credit. Halley did use the principles to predict the orbit and return of the comet that would later bear his name, but it was only after his death that he received any acclaim. And because Halley's Comet only returns once every seventy-six years, the mention of Edmund Halley is rather occasional. Halley remained a devoted scientist who did not care who received the credit as long as the cause was being advanced.[2]

When one sets the life of Samson alongside the life of Jesus, the contrast could not be starker. Samson was self-centered; Jesus was other-centered. Samson was driven by his passions; Jesus resisted his temptations in order to do what was right. Samson used people for his own ends; Jesus saw people as ends in and of themselves. Samson used his gifts of charisma, humor and strength to get what he wanted; Jesus used his gifts of charisma, healing and teaching for the benefit of others. God could use Samson, but only in a limited way; God used Jesus fully for the sake of humanity. Samson trivialized his God-given gifts for himself; Jesus honored his Heavenly Father by utilizing his gifts for others.

What gifts have we received from God? What are we doing with those gifts? God's purposes in this world are too important and his plans are too significant to trifle them away on ourselves.

PRAYER: Lord God, we are thankful and somewhat worried at the same time. We are thankful for the gifts you have given to us. We know we have so received them because of your love and

2   http://www.sermonillustrations.com/a-z/s/selflessness.htm

care. Yet, we confess that sometimes we worry because we are not sure we want to use our gifts in the way you desire. We do not want to be like Samson, but we find it easier to live selfishly. We do want to be like Jesus, but we find it harder to live focused on others. By the power of your Holy Spirit, assist us as we seek to live in all ways for your honor and glory; in Jesus' name. Amen.

10
This Is Our King!
(1 SAMUEL 10:19-24)

Dr. James Mayfield, the pastor at Tarrytown United Methodist Church in Austin, Texas talks about what it means to be "snake bit."

"From time to time when I was growing up, I would hear my grandfather speak of someone as being 'snake bit.' I knew he was not talking about an encounter with a rattlesnake. He was talking about the way someone encountered life. Folks who were "snake bit" were folks whose past choices had placed them in bad situations, where they made more bad choices which placed them in more bad situations." To be "snake bit," Mayfield says, is to be a person whose decisions in life keep one from moving in the right direction in life.[1]

The people of Israel are snake bit. God continues to lead them and provide for them, and yet, even though God has now brought them into the land of Canaan, into the Promised Land where they have settled, living in a place they can call home, the people still believe they know better, and they make decisions that leave them snake bit.

The people of Israel are the people of God. This meant that they are not to be like all the other nations. They are different. They are unique. One aspect of their uniqueness is that, since God is their king, they are to have no earthly monarch like all the other nations. But they were unable to trust in the One who had led them through the wilderness and protected them

---

1   James Mayfield, "More Stories about Grace: Good News for Snake Bit People." http://www.tarrytownumc.org/sermons/sr20030316.htm

through the years. They began to clamor to God's prophet Samuel, "We want a king like all the other nations." Somehow it was reasoned that a human king was better than a divine one. Eventually God relented giving the people what they wanted, and saying to Samuel, "They have not rejected you; they have rejected me."

And does God give them the king they want? Saul looks like a king. He is head and shoulders taller than everyone else and he is quite good looking. All of us have images in our own minds of how a true leader should look. Saul fits the image perfectly. Had he lived some three thousand years later, he could have been a general on a modern battlefield. Saul looks the part of royalty. He looks like a warrior. Our Old Testament lesson tells us "They ran and brought him out, and as he stood among the people he was a head taller than any of the others. Samuel said to all the people, 'Do you see the man the LORD has chosen? There is no one like him among all the people.'"

Then the people shouted, "This is our king!"

Be careful what you ask for, you just might get it. The people get what they ask for, but what they discover over time, is that while Saul may look the part, he is not fit for it. Saul is ruthless, he undermines his own people, he acts to preserve his own power, he opposes the priests, and he attempts to thwart the very plans of God—to make David the king in his place. Indeed, the people of Israel have received exactly what they asked for—they have a king like all the other nations.

But even though the people had rejected God in their desire for a king, God had not rejected his people. One thing we must always remember is that God works with us and in spite of us. God continues to lead and move when things go according to God's plan, and when they don't. God will use Saul as Israel's king, even though God wanted to be their king. God will lead his people even though they prefer to be led by Saul. Even when we find that our lives have become snake bit, whether by our own bad decisions, or through circumstances over which we have no control, God will not abandon his people and leave them—leave us—to ourselves.

The following is a true story from Reader's Digest. On January 10, 1948, just two years after the end of the Second World War, Marcel Sternberger took a train in the Brooklyn subway.[2] Usually, he took a different line, but his schedule changed because he wanted to visit a sick friend that morning. So now he was on a different train departing at noon so he could get to work. Sternberger stepped on the train and it was packed. He was just getting ready to get off to wait for the next train, when one man suddenly jumped from his seat and left the train hurriedly, probably realizing at the last minute that he was about to miss his stop. Sternberger took the vacant seat. Sitting next to him was a man reading a Hungarian newspaper. Sternberger was born in Hungary and though he was not the type of person to start a conversation with strangers, he felt compelled to do so. He turned to the man and said in Hungarian, "I hope you don't mind if I glance at your paper." The man was surprised to be addressed in his native language. During their trip they began to talk.

The man began to share with Sternberger his heartrending story. His last name was Paskin. When the war started, he was a law student. Eventually, he was enlisted in a labor battalion and sent to the Ukraine. He was captured by the Russians and was put to work burying the German dead. After the war was over, he travelled hundreds of miles on foot to return to his home in Debrecen, Hungary, only to discover that his entire family was gone. Strangers were living in the apartment he had once occupied with his father, mother, brothers, and sisters. When he reached his apartment where he had lived with his wife, it was also occupied by people he did not know. Finally, he found some old

---

2   As told in Paul Deutschman, "It Happened on the Brooklyn Subway," *Reader's Digest* (May 1949), 45-48. See also Bill T. Arnold, *1 & 2 Samuel. NIV Application Commentary* (Grand Rapids: Zondervan, 2003.

friends in Debrecen who had survived the carnage of the war. They sorrowfully informed him that his entire family was dead. The Nazis had taken them and his wife to Auschwitz where they were presumably murdered in the gas chambers.

Paskin was shocked by the news. He left Hungary, which was now to him a land of death. He went west toward Paris and eventually he emigrated to the United States in October of 1947. As Sternberger listened to the man's incredible story, somehow it seemed familiar, and suddenly it dawned on him. Only recently, he had met a young woman in the home of friends who had also been from Debrecen. She had been taken to Auschwitz, but was then transferred to work in a German munitions factory. All her relatives had been killed in the gas chambers. After she and the camp had been liberated by the Americans, she was brought to New York in the first boatload of Displaced Persons in 1946. Sternberger had been so stirred by her story he had written down her address and phone number, hoping to invite her to meet his family in order to assist her in her time of loneliness and grief.

Sternberger could not imagine that this was nothing more than a strange coincidence, but when the train reached his stop, he stayed on the subway with his newfound friend. Sternberger asked Paskin informally, "Is your first name "Bela?""

The man's face went pale—"Yes! How did you know?"

Sternberger fumbled for his address book, as he asked, "Was your wife's name Marya?"

Looking as though he might pass out, Paskin said, "Yes! Yes!"

Sternberger suggested that they get off at the next station without explanation. He led Paskin to a nearby phone booth. While Paskin stood there like a man in a stupor, Sternberger made a phone call, and after what seemed like an eternity, Sternberger had Marya Paskin on the line. Sternberger reminded her of their recent chance meeting, and she remembered him. Without explaining why, Sternberger asked where Marya had lived in Debrecen before the war. She told him the address. Sternberger turned to Paskin and asked, "Did you and your wife live on such-and-such street?"

"Yes!" Bela exclaimed, as he trembled.

Sternberger urged Paskin to stay calm, but then readied him by telling him the miraculous was about to happen. Then he handed Bela the phone, saying, "Here, take this telephone and talk to your wife."

When Paskin realized that he was actually speaking with his Marya, he cried uncontrollably. Sternberger sent him by taxi to be reunited with his wife. Bela and Marya each thought the other was dead; and now half-way across the world in their new country, they were husband and wife once again.

Reader's Digest ends the article in this way:

"Skeptical persons would no doubt attribute the events of that afternoon to mere chance. But was it chance that made Sternberger suddenly decide to visit his sick friend, and hence take a subway line that he had never been on before? Was it chance that caused the man sitting by the door of the car to rush out just as Sternberger came in? Was it chance that caused Bela Paskin to be sitting beside Sternberger, reading a Hungarian newspaper? Was it chance—or did God ride the Brooklyn subway that afternoon?"

Was the aggression of Nazi Germany God's will? Were the Holocaust, Auschwitz, and gas chambers divinely ordained? Of course not! But even when we human beings do our worst, God is in the mix of our misdeeds performing his best. In the midst of the godless horror of what happened in Europe many decades ago, that affected a town in Hungary, Bela and Marya Paskin were reminded after the war that God had not stopped working and leading and offering goodness in a world that, for a while, had gone insane. Israel's rebellious desire for a king would not thwart God's plans to lead Israel to the place where Israel's Messiah,

Jesus, would offer salvation to the world; and because of Jesus, God continues to insert himself into the muddle of our affairs working and leading and bringing his goodness and love, when we are faithful, when we are not, and even when life hurls more garbage at us than we can imagine.

Before his ascension to heaven, Jesus reminded us that he would be with us always. That is one truth we can count on in today's world.

PRAYER: Lord God, in this day, help us to be sensitive to the possibility that our circumstances may be more than coincidence. Assist us in discerning that in our conversations, we may be speaking your word. Prod us to move perhaps to places we had not planned on traveling. Amen.

11
Is This Our King?
(1 SAMUEL 16:1-13)

A New York City businessman decided to avoid a $20 service charge by replacing a fluorescent light himself. After he had smuggled a new light into his office and put it in place, he decided to get rid of the old tube by throwing it in the trash can near his subway stop. That night he got on the subway holding the seven-foot light vertically, with one end resting on the floor of the car and the top of the light touching the roof of the car, wedging the light somewhat firmly in place. As the train became more crowded other passengers took hold of the tube, assuming it was a brace. By the time the man reached his stop, he simply removed his hand and exited the car, leaving the other passengers gripping the fluorescent tube![1] Can we imagine the surprise when a sudden jerk of the subway caused that fluorescent light to come loose creating a domino effect of people falling into each other?

No doubt, the people of Israel got a real surprise when David was anointed king over Israel. No one was surprised that Saul was anointed king. He was tall and good-looking; an imposing figure on the battlefield. When he was anointed, the people in great certainty affirmed that the right man had been chosen, shouting, "*This* is our king!" But this was not the way it was with David. When he finally stands before the people, they are probably asking themselves, "Is *this* our king?"

As Samuel prepares to go to the family of a man named Jesse, God advises Samuel of words that should have been heeded when Saul was anointed, "Do not consider his appearance or his height, for I have rejected him. The Lord does not consider important

---

1   *Today in the Word* Chicago: Moody, June 24, 1992.

the things humans think are significant. Human beings look at the outward appearance, but the Lord looks at the heart" (1 Samuel 16:17 NIV).

When Samuel reaches the home of Jesse, a ritual begins in which each of his sons is paraded past Samuel. Abinadab, who is the oldest and, therefore the expected choice, is not the one. This no doubt surprised those standing around who lived in a culture where it was customary to crown as king those of first-born status. But as each son stands in front of Samuel, each son is rejected. Samuel knows that God has not chosen any he has seen.

There must be another. Samuel inquires of Jesse. Yes, there is the youngest, but he is tending the sheep. Jesse didn't even consider that David might be the choice. He was likely in his late teenage years, and unlike Saul and David's brother Abinadab, he did not look the part of a monarch.

But Samuel is adamant. David must be brought before him. As David arrives, the description given by the biblical writer reveals why his own family did not consider him to be a candidate. "He was ruddy, with a fine appearance and handsome features." Most English translations do not capture the implications of the Hebrew. Although the language is somewhat vague, a better way to translate this conceptually was that David had a fair complexion, with beautiful eyes, and he was pretty. Now having a fair complexion would not be considered out of the ordinary in Scandinavia, but in a Mediterranean and Semitic culture, he would have stood out as quite different. In addition, the reference to his eyes and his appearance suggest to us that David's features were almost feminine. His looks were soft and slight. Some translations may read that David was handsome, but it is more correct to say that he was almost pretty, which is not something any man wants to hear about himself. Many years ago, Hollywood made a movie about King David, with Richard

Gere, playing the main role. The real King David did not look like Richard Gere!

But God does not look upon the appearance. The people looked upon Saul's appearance and considered him fit for the job; now they look upon David's appearance and wonder what God is thinking. God removed his approval from Saul because of Saul's unfaithfulness to God and to the covenant; David will reign, not in perfection, but in sincere faith. He will become, as the Scripture tells us, "a man after God's own heart" (1 Samuel 13:14).

What we so often think and what we so often mark as the measure of a man or woman can be deceiving. It's not that we are always wrong about people and their abilities, but we know that too often our judgments about people are based more on what we perceive than what we actually know. Our evaluations of others can be so superficial. But God gets to the heart of the matter. David did not look like a king, but God knew that he had the heart that was fit for a king of Israel. And throughout his reign David would demonstrate the truth of what God knew. Long after David's death, and prior to the birth of Jesus, the people of Israel, her leaders, and her prophets would hold up King David as the standard for faithful rule, and he would be the template for that new king, the Messiah, the Anointed One, who would come to restore Israel's fortunes once and for all.

Neither would that new King David, Jesus, fit the part by human appearances either. He was born in a small village and his parents were simple peasants attempting to carve out enough of an existence simply to put food on the table. Jesus was not trained at a rabbinic school, and he was from Galilee, not a place that would have been considered acceptable geography to the religious gatekeepers. Even though Jesus was descended from David, throughout his ministry many simply could not accept that this son of David was the one God had chosen to deliver the people. The people's perspective was too narrow, too human.

In *How Life Imitates the World Series*, Dave Bosewell tells a story about Earl Weaver, former manager of the Baltimore Orioles and perhaps his most famous player, Reggie Jackson.

Weaver had a rule that no one could steal a base unless given the steal sign. This upset Jackson because he felt he knew the pitchers and catchers well enough to judge who he could and could not steal off of. So one game Jackson decided to steal without a sign.

He got a good jump off the pitcher and easily beat the throw to second base. As he shook the dirt off his uniform, Jackson smiled with delight, feeling he had vindicated his judgment to his manager.

Later Weaver took Jackson aside and explained why he hadn't given the steal sign. First, the next batter was Lee May, his best power hitter other than Jackson. When Jackson stole second, first base was left open, so the other team walked May intentionally, taking the bat out of his hands.

Second, the following batter hadn't been strong against that pitcher, so Weaver felt he had to send up a pinch hitter to try to drive in the men on base. That left Weaver without bench strength later in the game when he needed it.

The problem Jackson had was that he saw only his relationship to the pitcher and catcher. Weaver was watching the whole game. Jackson's vision was limited, Weaver's was much larger. Jackson was focused on the brief moment; Weaver had his eyes on the entire game.

The people of Israel were so focused on what they saw as their momentary needs, that they judged King Saul as a real king based on their narrow perspective. No doubt with that same limited view, they questioned, at first, David's ability to lead. But in the midst of the fleeting moments of life there is always more going on, and judgment is best rendered, not by appearances, but in the heart and the soul of the faithful. Jesus too was judged unfit by those who thought they knew better, by those who judged by outward appearances; but just as God chose David, so God also called Jesus.

As Old Testament scholar, Bill Arnold states,

"Looks, indeed, can be deceiving, and often are. Samuel needs help in learning to see God's perspective regarding David. Likewise, we need a God-perspective in order to overcome our biases. We often fail to see the God potential in others (or in ourselves) because we are easily impressed by the wrong indicators. David, who will become the ideal anointed figure, is an unassuming sort when we first meet him. He would not have naturally attracted attention as a potential savior of his people…. When you and I consider the qualities of the people around us, we are inevitably (and inescapably) influenced by what we see with our eyes. But God sees things we miss. Because he has superior vision, we may often be surprised by the people he chooses to accomplish his purposes."[2]

God's ways are not our ways, God does not measure us superficially; God gets to the heart of the matter judging us on the substance of our character and the integrity of our faithfulness. We can do no less for others.

PRAYER: Gracious God, give us your large vision for this world and toward those around us. Forgive us for when we have judged others through the superficial lenses of our humanity, and help us to see all persons from your divine perspective. May we remember that you do not need advice from us on whom to call and how to accomplish your will in this world. May we also learn to see others, not through our human eyes, but from your divine perspective. Amen.

---

2   Arnold, *1 & 2 Samuel*, 233, 235-236.

12
Living Wisely
(1 KINGS 3:1-28)

Isaac Asimov, familiar to many as a noted scientist and author, once told a story about a Rabbi Feldman who was having trouble with his congregation. It seemed they could agree upon nothing. The president of the congregation said, "Rabbi, this cannot be allowed to continue. Come, there must be a conference, and we must settle all areas of dispute once and for all." The rabbi agreed.

At the appointed time, the rabbi, the president, and ten elders met in the conference room of the synagogue, sitting around a magnificent mahogany table. One by one the issues were dealt with and on each issue, it became more and more apparent that the rabbi was a lonely voice in the wilderness. The president of the synagogue said, "Come, Rabbi, enough of this. Let us vote and allow the majority to rule." He passed out the slips of paper and each man made his mark. The slips were collected and the president said, "You may examine them, Rabbi. It is eleven to one against you. We have the majority."

The rabbi rose to his feet and said, "You now think because of the vote that you are right and I am wrong. Well, that is not so. The rabbi raised his arms impressively. "I call upon the Holy One of Israel to give us a sign that I am right and you are wrong." And as he said this, there came a frightful crack of thunder and a brilliant flash of lightning that struck the mahogany table and cracked it in two. The room was filled with smoke and fumes, and the president and the elders were hurled to the floor. Through the carnage and the rubble, the rabbi remained standing straight and untouched, his eyes flashing and a smile on his face. Slowly, the president lifted himself above what was left of the table. His hair was singed, his glasses were hanging from one ear and his clothing was in disarray. Finally he said, "All right, eleven to two. But we still have the majority."[1]

Wisdom is not necessarily tied to majority rule, nor is divine wisdom always revealed so clearly and so dramatically. Wisdom has been sought after by people of character for centuries. In the ancient world, good kings wanted to be known for their wisdom. It was common for monarchs to publish wisdom sayings, much like what we read in the book of Proverbs. To have a king, who was also a sage, was considered a blessing to his people.

In our Old Testament lesson, Solomon, the new and novice king, realizes the gravity of the office he now holds. He has immense power at his command. He could have treated his authority haphazardly, immediately using it for his own selfishness. He could have asked God to bless him with wealth; he could have desired long life in a world where it was not uncommon for kings to die young. Instead, in the knowledge that the role of the King of Israel was larger than he was, in the admission that he had no idea what he was doing, Solomon asks God for a discerning heart. Solomon asks for wisdom.

Ancient kings had a judicial role. They were expected to administer justice. One of the Psalms states, "Give the king your justice, O God, and your righteousness to a king's son. May he judge your people in righteousness, and your poor with justice. May the mountains yield prosperity for the people, and the hills in righteousness" (72:1-3).

"Prosperity and peace are possible only when there is justice."[2] As the king goes so goes the nation. Justice for the people is only possible when the king acts justly.

---

1   http://www.spirit-net.ca/sermon.html
2   August H. Konkel, *1 & 2 Kings. The NIV Application Commentary.* (Grand Rapids: Zondervan, 2006), 83.

It isn't long before Solomon gets his first opportunity to administer justice. Two women stand before him, each claiming the same baby. There is no way to know, based on any kind of evidence or eyewitness testimony, who is telling the truth. It is a case of one word against another.

Both women are prostitutes. In Solomon's day, a woman took up prostitution for basically one of two reasons: she was a widow who had no financial support from members of her family, or she was sold into prostitution as a young girl by her parents; something that is still sadly happening in our world in the twenty-first century. These are women who have nothing, and so to have a child to care for gave each of them something to look forward to day after day; and it also gave them something to love in a world of daily physical contact but no true human affection.

One of these mothers has lost her baby by accidentally smothering it in her sleep. Each claims the living child as hers. There is no way to corroborate the story of either woman. Solomon must draw on his wisdom if justice is to be served.

Since there is no way to discover the truth evidentially, Solomon orders that the living child be cut in two and half given to each woman. The Law of Moses provides for the division of disputed property under certain circumstances. This is not a decision that can be appealed. The king's word is law.

Solomon, knowing that loving parents would sooner sacrifice their own needs and wants than that of their children, is not surprised when the real mother offers to give up her child, so that the baby will be spared. Solomon exercises wisdom even though he has no knowledge of the details of what exactly happened. Solomon is discerning even though he is ignorant of how the events that led to a child's death unfolded.

Too often we confuse wisdom with knowledge. They are not the same and the Bible says as much. One can have much knowledge and still act foolishly; one can be quite uneducated and live wisely. This is not to say that knowledge is unimportant. It is a good thing for a surgeon to know anatomy before she operates on a patient. But wisdom is more than knowledge. Wisdom discerns what is true even when knowledge fails.

For the Bible, one cannot have wisdom without first and foremost trusting in God. It is God himself who is wisdom, and living wisely means trusting God each day as we live in God's world. In Genesis chapter three in the story of the Garden of Eden, Adam and Eve are told not to eat of the tree of the knowledge of good and evil quite simply because they do not have the wisdom to employ that knowledge rightly. Human history has demonstrated that we still struggle to employ divine wisdom as we utilize the knowledge we have. In 1997 on the second anniversary of the shooting at Columbine High School, a student wrote the following, which I have edited.

> The paradox of our time in history is that we have taller buildings, but shorter tempers; Wider freeways, but narrower viewpoints; We spend more, but have less; We buy more, but enjoy it less. We have bigger houses, but smaller families; More conveniences, but less time; We have more degrees, but less sense; More knowledge, but less judgment; More experts, but more problems; More medicine, but less wellness. We have multiplied our possessions, but reduced our values. We talk too much, love too seldom, and hate too often. We've learned how to make a living, but not a life; We've added years to life, but not life to years. We've been to the moon and back, but have trouble crossing the street to meet the new neighbor. We've conquered outer space, but not inner space; We've cleaned up the air, but polluted the soul; We've split the atom, but not our prejudice. We have higher incomes, but lower morals; We've become long on quantity, but short on quality. These are the times of tall men and short character; Steep profits and shallow relationships.

It is a time when there is much in the showroom
and nothing in the stockroom.

In other words, we struggle to live wisely; and we have put
our trust and our future into our hands, instead of in the hands
of God.

If God could grant us one desire, what would it be? What
would we ask for? Would we ask for wealth? Long life? Or would
we, like Solomon, ask for what is necessary to live a truly abundant
life of joy and virtue, no matter how long or short that life might
be? Do we desire a life of wisdom?

But divine wisdom will not simply be rained down from heaven
upon us with no effort on our part. Like Solomon we must ask
so that God will grant it to us, but then we must utilize the
wisdom we have received. Solomon's life will take a sad turn,.
Later on in his life it will become all too clear that Solomon rejects
that divine wisdom he has received. After that first wise decision
early in his reign, Solomon fails time after time to employ what
had been given to him as a gift. It is true that God will give us
wisdom, but we must also seek it.

The Book of Proverbs states that wisdom calls to us from the
streets imploring us to listen. Are we listening? Are we seeking?
Are we living wisely?

PRAYER: Gracious God, make us wise not in our own
understanding, but in your truth. Give us the faith to seek that
truth wherever it may be, and may we rejoice when we find it. We
ask this in the name of Jesus Christ our Lord, Savior, and your
wisdom come to earth. Amen.

13
Divine Senses
(2 KINGS 20:1-11)

Five year old Johnny was in the kitchen as his mother made supper. She asked him to go into the pantry and get her a can of tomato soup, but he didn't want to go in alone. "It's dark in there and I'm scared." She asked again, and he persisted. Finally she said, "It's OK—Jesus will be in there with you." Johnny walked hesitantly to the door and slowly opened it. He peeked inside, saw it was dark, and started to leave when all at once an idea came, and he said: "Jesus, if you're in there, would you hand me that can of tomato soup?"[1]

We all have fears. Some of them are understandable, others are irrational; but I think most of us can relate to the fear King Hezekiah must have experienced when the Prophet Isaiah informed him of the word of the Lord that he would die and not recover from his illness.

Hezekiah was by no means a perfect king, but he was one of Israel's good kings. Hezekiah reigned over the southern kingdom of Judah during the late eighth and early seventh centuries B.C. He introduced many religious reforms and reinstituted religious traditions that had been lost or rejected. Just a few years before his ascent to the throne, the Assyrian Empire destroyed the northern kingdom of Israel in 722 B.C. creating a huge refugee problem for the kingdom of Judah. Hezekiah not only had to deal with that, but he also sought to throw off the dependence Judah had on the more powerful Assyrians.

---

1   http://www.sermonillustrations.com/a-z/f/fear.htm

In our Old Testament lesson, King Hezekiah has become ill with an unidentified skin condition. Skin maladies of various sorts were prevalent in the ancient world, and some of them could be deadly. Whatever the exact nature of the king's illness, the Lord comes to Isaiah for the purpose of informing the king that he will not recover. Prophets were not only the bearers of glad tidings, but also of bad news.

As Hezekiah laid there in the silence, we are told that he turned his face toward the wall and prayed, "Remember, O LORD, how I have walked before you faithfully and with wholehearted devotion and have done what is good in your eyes" (2 Kings 20:3 NIV).

It is difficult to ascertain from this prayer what Hezekiah is asking God for. He does not specifically request to be healed, although perhaps he hopes God will look upon his reign as one of religious reformation and perhaps heal him on account of his faithfulness. We are not sure, but Hezekiah certainly wants God to look upon him with favor as one who has been a faithful servant.

Hezekiah turns his face toward the wall. Perhaps the king is not alone, having many servants to attend to him and court officials always at hand. Perhaps Hezekiah doesn't want those in the room with him to see him in a vulnerable moment. Maybe the king is indeed alone and in turning his face toward the wall, he unconsciously acts in a symbolic way to face the "wall" that has just been thrown in front of his life's journey. Whatever the situation, it is difficult to know what someone is thinking when one cannot see his or her face. Hezekiah is indeed alone with his thoughts and his sorrows and his fear.

Dr. Daniel Boorstin was the Librarian of Congress from 1975 until 1987. Many years ago, about halfway through a PBS program on the Library of Congress, Boorstin brought out a little blue box from a small closet that once held the library's rarities. The label on the box read: *Contents of the President's Pockets on the Night of*

April 14, 1865. Since that was the fateful night Abraham Lincoln was assassinated, it was obvious that the box contained the contents of Abraham Lincoln's pockets the night of his murder. Boorstin then proceeded to remove the items in the small container and display them on camera. There were five things in the box: a handkerchief, embroidered "A. Lincoln," a country boy's pen knife, a spectacles case repaired with string, a purse containing a $5.00 Confederate bill, and some old and worn newspaper clippings.

"The clippings," said Boorstin, "were concerned with the great deeds of Abraham Lincoln. One of them actually reported on a speech by one John Bright which stated that Abraham Lincoln was "one of the greatest men of all times.""[2]

It is generally believed today that Lincoln was one of the great individuals of history and one of the greatest presidents in U.S. history. The world now knows that British statesman Bright was correct in his assessment of Lincoln, but in 1865 millions shared a very different opinion. The President's critics were fierce and many. His was a lonely agony that reflected the suffering and turmoil of his country ripped to shreds by hatred and a cruel, costly war. Some have suggested that Lincoln carried those newspaper clippings because he was somewhat stuck on himself and wanted to read the words of those who gave him such wonderful accolades; but most agree that he carried such words with him for encouragement in the midst of a hostile environment where Lincoln was vilified by the South, and castigated by the North for his inability to conclude the war sooner, and a press that regularly characterized him as a buffoon.

In the midst of the loneliness of his office, because of the times in which he served, Lincoln carried with him encouraging reminders of the few voices, who at the time were in the minority, but who now history has demonstrated were right.

---

2   Charles Swindoll, *The Quest For Character* (Grand Rapids: Zondervan), 62-3.

Hezekiah was a good king, but he no doubt had plenty of detractors as he attempted to deal with the Israelite refugee problem, and he clearly made enemies in the institution of his religious reforms; and now in the loneliness of these moments as he turns his face toward the wall facing his own death, he, like Abraham Lincoln reading newspaper clippings, needs to be reminded that he has been faithful, that he has done his best.

His prayer touches the heart of God. As Isaiah is leaving the king's court, God speaks to the prophet once again. "Go back and tell Hezekiah, the leader of my people, 'This is what the LORD, the God of your father David, says: I have heard your prayer and seen your tears; I will heal you. On the third day from now you will go up to the temple of the LORD. I will add fifteen years to your life. And I will deliver you and this city from the hand of the king of Assyria. I will defend this city for my sake and for the sake of my servant David'" (2 Kings 20:6 NIV).

God hears our prayers. I believe that. I resist any attempt to define prayer as just a psychological exercise that makes us feel better. Yes, we may indeed feel better after we go to God in prayer, but prayer is more than a psychological exercise. God hears us when we pray. To be sure, we may not always get the answer to our prayers that we desire. Sometimes, God says "yes," other times, "no," and at other times, "wait" or "maybe." Why God answers prayer in the way God does is beyond me. God is God and I am not. But I do know that God hears us when we pray; and prayer is a powerful thing.

While very ill, John Knox, the founder of the Presbyterian Church in Scotland, called to his wife and said, "Read me that Scripture where I first cast my anchor." After he listened to the beautiful prayer of Jesus recorded in John 17, he seemed to forget his weakness. He began to pray, interceding, not for himself, but for others. He prayed for those who did not know Jesus. He pleaded on behalf of people who were new converts. And he requested protection for those in full-time Christian service, many of whom were facing persecution. At one point while Knox was praying, his voice fell silent. The man of whom Queen Mary had said, "I fear his prayers more than I do the armies of my enemies," ministered through prayer until the moment of his death.

God not only hears our prayers, but God sees our tears, even when no one else does, even when our face is to the wall. Two thousand years ago, God became flesh and lived in our world. As a human being, Jesus Christ, God in the flesh, experienced everything we experience. He knew the joys of family and friends and he experienced laughter during humorous moments. He experienced the refreshment of a good night's sleep and the satisfaction of eating a home-cooked meal. Jesus also knew the grief of losing family and friends to death. He experienced disappointment when people he loved let him down. He knew the great pain of emotional and physical suffering; and he experienced what all of us will encounter sooner or later—our own deaths.

No matter what we go through in this life—the joys and sorrows, the happiness and sadness, the experience of life and death—because God has become flesh in Jesus Christ and has lived among us in this world, the one thing we cannot say to God is, "You do not know what it is like." God does know what it is like; God sees our tears and they touch his very heart because a long time ago, when God dwelt on this earth, he cried too.

God saw King Hezekiah's tears and heard his prayer. The Bible promises that God also sees our tears and hears our prayers. How God will answer each individual prayer we offer, I cannot say, but God's divine senses are in tune with each and every one of us. God knows what we experience, even when those around us do not. God understands what we feel, even when those we love have trouble understanding our fears. And God knows better than anyone else, what we need; for God not only knows of our need in Jesus Christ, but he is able to meet our need in ways neither we nor anyone else can. And sometimes what we need is different from what we want. There are times that we do not know how to separate the two, but God is always able.

God's divine senses are in tune with us, knowing our need even before we ask.

PRAYER: Lord God, hear our prayers this day. Answer according to what is best for us, knowing as we say this, that what we want is not always best, and what we need can be different from what we think; in the name of Jesus Christ our Lord and Savior. Amen.

14

On Keeping the Main Thing the Main Thing
(2 CHRONICLES 34-8-21)

Several years ago on a Saturday, my siblings, I and our families went to our parents' house for a good spring cleaning. We had recently placed my father in a nursing home, and my mom wanted things gone through, with much that was accumulated over the years, thrown out. So we rented a huge dumpster and began our work.

As we went through the stuff that was in the garage, I opened a weathered produce box and there found old newspapers that my father had saved through the years. As I glanced through each paper, it was obvious why he saved them. One newspaper was published the day after John F. Kennedy's assassination. Another one was dated July of 1969 and carried the news of the landing of the Apollo 11 with Neil Armstrong's first ever moonwalk by a human being. There were some other papers saved because they reported events that captured transcendent moments—the kinds of moments that, whether they were triumphs or tragedies—forced us as Americans out of the normal and narrow focus of the day's routine to remind us that life in general was larger than our individual lives, that something bigger was afoot in this world of which we were all a small part.

History is replete with such times—moments that plead for us to look beyond ourselves in order to see something larger. These are events that are replayed in history, that are not forgotten amidst the clutter of all the world's happenings. They are moments that seem to be junctures in history, dramatic occurrences that seem to beckon us, indeed almost scream for us to remember. To forget these pivotal times would be immoral, for they are events that help shape our identity and force us to see a larger picture of reality.

We remember such moments in American history and we tell them to each new generation: the signing of the Declaration of Independence, Abraham Lincoln's Gettysburg Address, Franklin Roosevelt's eloquent and confident speech to Congress and the nation the day after the attack on Pearl Harbor, John F. Kennedy's sobering and resolute words during the Cuban Missile Crisis, the "I Have a Dream Speech" from Martin Luther King, Jr., and Ronald Reagan's challenge to the President of the Soviet Union as he addressed the people of West Berlin, "Mr. Gorbachev, tear down this wall." And how many of us watched the television a little over two years later in 1990, as Berliners, East and West, piece by piece with hammers and chisels destroyed what had become one of the most visible and enduring symbols of Communism. And, of course, we cannot forget 9/11 and the video of George W. Bush standing on the rubble of the World Trade Center addressing the workers given the grim task of searching for victims and clearing away debris; and the President with his arm around one of those laborers offering words of inspiration with bullhorn in hand. And most recently, we witnessed the election of the first African American President of the United States, something that would have been unimaginable just a few years ago.

There are transcendent moments that take us out of ourselves and remind us that we are more than the sum of our individual parts. There are times when certain things transpire that are so loaded with profound meaning, that we remember once again that we are more than Democrats and Republicans, liberals and conservatives, Methodists and Presbyterians. There are times when we realize that something bigger is afoot in this world and such occasions give us pause, a moment in which partisanship gives way to reflection, politics stands behind philosophy, and the day's routine moves into the shadow of history.

With all this in mind, is it possible to relate to the transcendent moment that takes place in our Old Testament lesson. Josiah is one of the good kings of Judah. He begins a series of religious reforms to reinstitute the worship of Israel's God in the land. Central to his reforms is the task of renovating Solomon's Temple which has fallen into severe disrepair. The worship of God has been neglected, so God's House has been neglected. As the day's routine of labor at the Temple is progressing, the priest Hilkiah finds the book of Law of Moses (what is probably the Book of Deuteronomy) that had long been lost and apparently forgotten. When the worship of God is neglected, God's word is disregarded.

And as Josiah hears the words of God's Law, the king is mortified. He realizes how far he and his people have strayed from the will of God, from the covenant that God made with Moses. It is one of those transcendent moments when the king and the people are forced to think beyond themselves, to realize that something bigger is afoot, something that not even the renovation of the Temple itself can capture. Down through the years, the kings and the people of Israel struggled to be faithful. How often they were so focused on themselves and the factions that gave this little group and that little group their identity that they could not see the larger picture of what God wanted to do through them as an entire people. In attending to themselves, they failed to attend to the ways of God and they lost focus. Scripture was neglected and even lost! As a result they failed to keep the main thing, faithfulness to God, as the main thing.

We human beings have a terrible habit of majoring in the minors. We get so focused on the small stuff that we lose the largeness of this world and God's workings in it. We spend so much time trivializing the momentous and complicating the obvious, we forget that we are not the center of the universe. And when we lose the central place of God in Jesus Christ in our lives, we fail to keep the main thing the main thing.

A Methodist pastor, who was a mentor and colleague of mine (and who passed away a just a few years ago), went to High School and graduated with the famed and legendary chair-throwing basketball coach, Bobby Knight. One day, my friend, who was also named Bob, started reminiscing about his high school days, and the conversation turned to Knight. Bob told me that when it came to basketball, Bobby Knight was the most disciplined and focused individuals he ever knew. After basketball practice was over for the day, Knight stayed at school in the gym and continued to shoot baskets and run patterns all by himself for hours, long after everyone else, including his coaches had gone home. He practiced for several hours each weekend, and in the summer, when Bob and the rest of his buddies were playing baseball at the park, Bobby Knight was also at the park, but he was not on the ball diamond; Bobby Knight was at the basketball court.

One cannot be a good basketball player without focusing on and attending to the fundamentals of playing the game in a disciplined way. We cannot be faithful disciples of Jesus Christ when we do not attend to the fundamentals of the practices of our faith, worship, study, prayer, and service. Without these things, we end up trivializing the momentous and complicating the obvious. We major in minors. We fail to keep the main thing the main thing; and we will not recognize the transcendent moments when they take place, the events that remind us something larger is afoot.

Today it is common for us to talk of setting our priorities right when we know we need discipline. Notice the use of the plural "priorities." We speak as if all our responsibilities need to be put in order of importance; once we do that, everything will work out alright. But centuries ago, Christians spoke, not of getting their priorities (plural) straight. They spoke of setting their priority (singular). The singular priority was God. If God was put first, then everything else would follow. What followed did not need to be ranked in order of importance. If God was the priority, then everything else would fall in place. The trivial would not become momentous, and the obvious would not be complicated. Put God first; the rest will work out fine.

This sounds much like Jesus in the Sermon on the Mount when he counsels us, "Seek first the Kingdom of God and his righteousness, and all these things will be given to you" (Matthew 6:33). Jesus also says not to worry about the trivialities of each day; for each day has enough trouble of its own. If we heed such words, we Christians will keep the main thing the main thing, and we will recognize each transcendent moment that beckons us to pause and remember that God has something much bigger afoot in this world and we are blessed to have a small part in his plan.

PRAYER: Teach us, Good Lord, to serve you as you deserve; to give and not to count the cost; to fight and not to heed the wounds; to labor and not to ask for any reward, except that of knowing that we do your will; through Jesus Christ Our Lord, Amen. – Ignatius of Loyola (1491-1556)

15
Timing Is Everything
(ESTHER 4:1-17)

How much of our lives do we spend doing the things that come during the normal routine of the day? The experts who have studied this kind of thing have drawn general conclusions:

An average American individual who is fifty years old has spent

16.4 years sleeping

17.8 years working

A little over 2 years walking

Almost 11 years in recreational activities

4 years eating

1.5 years sick

7 years traveling

3 years getting dressed

An individual who is fifty years old has also

Eaten 17,000 pounds of bread

And 16,000 pounds of meat

4,600 pounds of vegetables, eggs, and fish

And drank 7,000 gallons of liquid (e.g. water, coffee, etc.)

Time passes by and moments move quickly. There is the passing of time and there is the time that matters. The Greeks had two words for time—*chronos*, and *kairos*. *Chronos* was the word used that referred to ordinary time, the movement from hour to hour and days to weeks. *Kairos* denoted special events and significant happenings. St. Paul uses *kairos* to refer to God's time. He tells the Galatians that when the time (*kairos*) had fully come, God sent his Son (4:4). In other words, Paul is stating that when the time was right, God sent his Son.

In the passing of time (*chronos*) there are divine moments that can only be described with the words kairos. Such is the case with our Old Testament lesson. The events of the book of Esther take place in the middle of the fifth century B.C. Esther is a young Jewish maiden who has been taken into the harem of King Ahasuerus by royal decree. Her cousin Mordecai, apparently concerned for her safety, advises Esther not to reveal her Jewish lineage to anyone including the king. Living in the king's palace concealing her identity meant that Esther had to live as a Persian. She had to eat things forbidden by Jewish law, she could not observe the holy days of her people, and she probably had to participate in religious rituals to pagan gods. Through no fault of her own, she was taken out of her world, with its sacred beliefs and practices, and she was forced to participate in a different world, one that the Jewish Law forbid to all of God's people.

Once she becomes queen, Esther keeps in contact with her cousin Mordecai, who raised Esther from the time she was a young girl. Mordecai has learned of a plot that has been hatched by the king's prime minister, Haman, to have the Jewish minority in Persia eradicated, the first of many attempts to exterminate God's people throughout history. Only Esther can save her people by warning the king about Haman's plot.

The risk to Esther was great. First, according to law, no one but the members of the king's inner court could approach the king unannounced, and this included even the queen. The penalty for entering the king's throne room unannounced was death. By law, Esther would have to petition for an audience with the king, and that could take days possibly weeks. Time was critical. Esther would have to take the risk and approach the king without petition. Second, even if the king looks past Esther's willful breaking of the law, she will have to inform him that she is Jewish, which could also bring his wrath down upon her, perhaps because of her ethnicity, and also possibly because she failed to disclose this to the king before they were married.

In any case, Esther finds herself in the midst of a difficult and dangerous situation. Mordecai is insistent that the reluctant Esther take the risk; the continued existence of her people in the capital city is at stake. And then Mordecai suggests to Esther in a message that she may be part of a kairos moment. "Do not think that in the king's palace you will escape any more than all the other Jews. For if you keep silence at such a time as this, relief and deliverance will rise for the Jews from another place, but you and your family will perish. Who knows? Perhaps you have come to royal dignity for just such a time as this" (4:13-14).

I am not a fatalist. I do not believe that God orchestrates every event and moment. I had a friend years ago who used to say that Christians don't believe in luck. Well, I am one Christian who does. I do not believe everything happens for a reason; in fact, I believe there are events that take place, which are senseless and cannot be attributed to anything profoundly divine. To be sure, God does use everything that happens for his purposes; out of the ashes of a catastrophe God can bring hope and life, and he will most certainly work his will in the midst of the chaos. But that does not mean that somehow God has foreordained every little thing that happens in life.

Yet, at the same time, I believe that God is intimately involved in this world's affairs. I believe that God is moving in our lives each and every day pushing and prodding and calling. Here is Esther, raised as a devout Jew and now forced to live her life as a pagan in the court of a pagan king. I doubt that it was God's will that she be forced into the breaking of the Law that God gave to his people Israel. But in the midst of her circumstances, here we see a divine moment, an opportunity for God to use her to save his people. Perhaps indeed her coming to the palace against her wishes will serve the greater purposes of God. Perhaps she has come to the palace for this kairos moment.

John Wesley's father, Samuel, was a dedicated pastor, but there were those in his parish who did not like him. On February 9, 1709, a fire broke out in the rectory at Epworth, possibly set by one of Samuel's enemies. Young John, not yet six years old, was stranded on an upper floor of the building. Two neighbors rescued the boy just seconds before the roof crashed in. One neighbor stood on another neighbor's shoulders and pulled young John through the window.

Samuel Wesley said, "Come, neighbors, let us kneel down. Let us give thanks to God. He has given me all my eight children. Let the house go. I am rich enough." John's mother, Suzanna, referred to her son as a "brand plucked from the burning" (Zechariah 3:2; Amos 4:11) who was spared for God's purposes. And God did use John Wesley in a mighty way.

Esther's life in the court of the king was set apart for this moment and now it was upon her. One has to admire her. Here was a young woman who had no say-so over her life, as most women in that time and place; and yet, for Esther it was even more so. Choices were made for her all of her life and now she is faced, for the first time, with a monumental decision, one that is a matter of life and death for her. And yet, she realizes that while she has a choice, honor and character demand that once again there is no option before her; she must go to the king, and risk herself for others. There are no other options and she knows that as she utters her last words to her uncle before going to see the king, "If I die, I die." Some things are worse than death. It is better to live a short and courageous life, than to have many years as a coward. Esther visits King Ahasuerus unannounced, he receives her, and Esther tells of Haman's plot, and she saves her people.

One summer morning as Ray Blankenship was preparing his breakfast, he gazed out the window, and saw a small girl being swept along in the rain-flooded drainage ditch beside his Andover, Ohio, home. Blankenship knew that farther downstream, the ditch disappeared with a roar underneath a road and then emptied into the main culvert. Ray dashed out the door and raced along the ditch, trying to get ahead of the foundering child. Then he hurled himself into the deep, churning water. Blankenship surfaced and was able to grab the child's arm. They tumbled end over end. Within about three feet of the yawning culvert, Ray's free hand felt something—possibly a rock—protruding from one bank. He clung desperately, but the tremendous force of the water tried to tear him and the child away. "If I can just hang on until help comes," he thought. He did better than that. By the time fire department rescuers arrived, Blankenship had pulled the girl to safety. Both were treated for shock. On April 12, 1989, Ray Blankenship was awarded the Coast Guard's Silver Lifesaving Medal. The award was fitting, for this selfless person was at even greater risk to himself than most people knew. Ray Blankenship couldn't swim.[1]

The brave person knows the kind of fear that the coward never will. Courage demands not options, not choices, but virtuous action, and acting rightly does not increase our options, but restricts them. Esther acted courageously in doing what she had to do, doing what virtue required; and it was a kairos moment, a moment which was much more than the passage of time. It was an event in which God was at work in her.

When Esther is wavering, Mordecai tells her that if she keeps silent, deliverance will come from another place. If Esther refuses to be God's instrument, God will raise up someone else. We must never think that God has only one way of fulfilling his will in our midst. Each and every day people refuse to be faithful; God calls and they will not to answer. God will find someone else. But why would we not want to answer the call of God? Why would we leave the task to someone else? Who knows, perhaps each and every one of us was called to our place, to our church, and to our community for such a time as this?

---

1   As told by the late Paul Harvey.

PRAYER: Gracious God, grant us faith for the journey, perseverance to stand the test, courage to act faithfully, and a willingness to hear your call in the divine moments of our days. Amen.

16
Curse God and Die
(JOB 2:1-13)

When Jewish psychiatrist Victor Frankl was arrested by the Nazis in World War II, he was stripped of everything—property, family, possessions. He had spent years researching and writing a book on the importance of finding meaning in life—concepts that later would be known as logo therapy. When he arrived in Auschwitz, the infamous death camp, even his manuscript, which he had hidden in the lining of his coat, was taken away.

"I had to undergo and overcome the loss of my spiritual child," Frankl wrote. "Now it seemed as if nothing and no one would survive me; neither a physical nor a spiritual child of my own! I found myself confronted with the question of whether under such circumstances my life was ultimately void of any meaning."

He was still wrestling with that question a few days later when the Nazis forced the prisoners to give up their clothes.

"I had to surrender my clothes and in turn inherited the worn-out rags of an inmate who had been sent to the gas chamber," said Frankl. "Instead of the many pages of my manuscript, I found in the pocket of the newly acquired coat a single page torn out of a Hebrew prayer book, which contained the main Jewish prayer, *Shema Yisrael* (Hear, O Israel! The Lord our God is one God. And you shall love the Lord your God with all your heart and with all your soul and with all your might.)

"How should I have interpreted such a 'coincidence' other than as a challenge to *live* my thoughts instead of merely putting them on paper?"

Later, as Frankl reflected on his ordeal, he wrote in his book *Man's Search for Meaning*, "There is nothing in the world that would so effectively help one to survive even the worst conditions, as the knowledge that there is a meaning in one's life . . "He who has a *why* to live for can bear almost any *how*.'"[1]

"He who has a *why* to live for can bear almost any *how*." Frankl's words are appropriate as one reads the book of Job. One can hardly read the first two chapters of the book and not feel sympathy, and perhaps some empathy, for this man who loses everything that means the most to him, and then suffers terribly in his own body.

In the beginning of the book Satan makes the case before God that Job is righteous and faithful because it is quite easy for him to be. If Job were here today, he could proudly wear one of those t-shirts that reads, "Life is good!" Job is blessed with a wonderful family and friends, great wealth, and he has the respect of everyone who knows him. Faithfulness is easy for those who are able to say, "Life is good!"

But if you actually want to discover who this guy truly is, just throw a little adversity his way. Several years ago, I spoke with a young man who basically abandoned his Christian faith because, as he said, it didn't keep him from losing his wife and his job. So what good was it?

Now Satan's argument does make some sense. The Bible itself tells us that trying times not only can produce character, but it can reveal one's character, or the lack thereof. It is certainly true, as Helen Keller wrote, "Character cannot be developed in ease and quiet. Only through experience of trial and suffering can the soul be strengthened, vision cleared, ambition inspired, and success achieved." But it is equally the case, to quote Booker T. Washington, that, "character, not circumstance, makes the person." Life is the workshop that develops character, but it is also the testing ground for character.

Job's character is tested. He encounters suffering that is almost indescribable in human terms. How will he react? His wife has

1   http://net.bible.org/illustration.php?id=7880

some clear convictions on how her husband should respond to the calamities he has experienced, "Curse God and die!" she says. Just before you take your last breath, Job, shake your fist at God. Don't give the Almighty the satisfaction of trying to convince you that somehow all this is your fault. God may have the last word, but you should at least get in a word. It's called protest.

In the spring of 1894, the Baltimore Orioles came to Boston to play a routine baseball game. But what happened that day was anything but routine. The Orioles' John McGraw got into a fight with the Boston third baseman. Within minutes all the players from both teams had joined in the brawl. The warfare quickly spread to the grandstands. Among the fans, the conflict went from bad to worse. Someone set fire to the stands and the entire ballpark burned to the ground. Not only that, but the fire spread to 107 other Boston buildings as well.[2]

That's what Job's wife wants Job to do—go out angry, and if you can, take God with you! Curse God and die! It is not easy to watch someone we love suffer terribly.

But Job has a different perspective. "Shall we accept the good from God, and not trouble?" When some encounter difficulty, they ask, "Why me?" When others experience calamity, they ask instead, "Why not me?"

We all know the obvious—good and bad are intrinsically part of our lives and our world this side of eternity. All of us experience both; none of us will be able to avoid either. To be sure, the Bible promises us that in Jesus Christ, God has made a way through our suffering, and one day, pain and even death itself will be defeated. In the meantime, however, the most significant question for us is not why we suffer, but how will we respond to suffering; and that is the question that concerns the book of Job. It is not, as many mistakenly assume, why bad things happen to good people, but rather how do good people respond to the suffering they encounter?

2   http://www.sermonillustrations.com/a-z/a/anger.htm

In November of 2006, Casey Coleman, Cleveland, Ohio sportscaster and one time radio voice of the Cleveland Browns, died at the age of 55, after a long illness. I remember the morning he died because I was actually driving home from a conference in Washington D.C. I had taken a detour on the way home to visit our daughter Alyssa, who was, at that time, attending college in North Carolina. As I was heading toward Ohio early in the morning, my radio was scanning and it stopped on WTAM out of Cleveland.

As I listened to the news of his death, and as his colleagues paid tribute to him, at one point, the station played an interview he had done only a month before his death. At one point he stated, that he decided when his illness was diagnosed that he could spend his remaining days in anger over the days and years he would not experience, or he could spend the rest of life in gratitude for the years he had received. In other words, Coleman refused to follow the advice of Job's wife to curse God and die. Instead he was grateful for the blessings he received from the hand of the Lord, even though he might have wished to receive those blessings a little longer.

Now, none of what I am saying suggests that we should take suffering and calamity lightly. There is no place for sentimental niceties and sweet clichés in the midst of the deep pains people experience. Of all people, Christians must not make light of the tragedy in our world. At the center of our faith stands the suffering of the cross; and like Jesus, his followers must be ready to enter into the suffering of those around them and of this world, just as Job's friends sat with him for seven days and seven nights, entering into his presence without saying a thing. And we are such a presence precisely because suffering is not the end of the Christian story. The tragedy of Good Friday leads to the victory of Easter. We enter into the suffering of others, and in so doing, we invite those who are in pain to enter into the hope we have received in Jesus Christ.

We receive life as a good gift from God. The appropriate response to God for the gift of life is one of gratitude. The appropriate posture in each day is not to curse God and die, but to bless the Lord each and every day that we live. Although the story of Job was written many centuries before Jesus was born, Job points us toward the truth that the worst that can happen to us in this world, cannot compare to the best that God has already accomplished for us in Jesus Christ.

The goodness of life is not to be measured by what we have not received, but in what God has graciously given to us, that by our blessings, we might bless those around us.

PRAYER: Gracious God, let us never forget that your Son suffered so much on our behalf. Remind us of this truth when we are suffering, that we might find comfort. Remind us of this truth when we see others suffering around us, that we might bring comfort to them; through the same Jesus Christ our Lord. Amen.

17
Let Someone Else Do It
(ISAIAH 6:1-13)

During the tenure of the great preacher and orator Henry Ward Beecher, a visiting minister (Beecher's brother) once substituted for the popular pastor. A large audience had already assembled to hear Beecher, and when the substitute pastor stepped into the pulpit, several disappointed listeners began to move toward the exits.

That's when the minister stood and said loudly, "All who have come here today to worship Henry Ward Beecher may now withdraw from the church. All who have come to worship God keep your seats!"[1]

We all know that God is at the center of our worship, but we freely admit as human beings that there are Sundays when we find it a challenge not to put ourselves as the focus of this time. We come wondering what God is going to do for us instead of thinking that God may actually want something from us.

But when God is at the center of worship, who knows what might happen on any given Sunday. In every instance in the Bible when someone encounters God, it is a life changing experience. Worship is comforting, uplifting, it gives us hope; it can also turn our world upside down. It is quite an awesome thing to enter into the presence of God.

United Methodist Bishop William Willimon says that if we Christians were truly open to the presence of God in our worship, and if we truly believed that God was going to move in our midst, then on Sunday morning instead of bulletins, the ushers would be handing out crash helmets.

---

1   http://www.sermonillustrations.com/a-z/w/worship_shapes_life.htm

The prophet Isaiah is in the temple worshiping when he has a crash helmet moment.

> *In the year that King Uzziah died, I saw the Lord seated on a throne, high and exalted, and the train of his robe filled the temple. Above him were seraphs, each with six wings: With two wings they covered their faces, with two they covered their feet, and with two they were flying. And they were calling to one another: "Holy, holy, holy is the LORD Almighty; the whole earth is full of his glory." At the sound of their voices the doorposts and thresholds shook and the temple was filled with smoke (Isaiah 1:1-4 NIV).*

"Christians should worship God in awe and wonder," said St. Cyril of Jerusalem. Apparently Isaiah has no choice but to worship God in this way.

Isaiah not only witnesses the grandeur of God, but God's holiness as well. In the world of the ancient Near East, the word "holy" was not extensively used, and it was a word that had no moral connotations. When Israel's neighbors used the term "holy" to describe their deities, they were simply affirming that their gods were not common. But for the Israelites, the notion of God as holy was very different. God's holiness not only meant that he was different from human beings, but that he was morally superior to human beings. His character was perfect and his actions were always just.

As Isaiah stands in the presence of this holy God, he realizes, perhaps as never before, that he is anything but holy. "Woe to me!" Isaiah shouts. "I am ruined! For I am a man of unclean lips, and I live among a people of unclean lips, and my eyes have seen the King, the LORD Almighty" (Isaiah 1:5 NIV).

On October 7, 1969 the Montreal, Canada police force went on strike. Because of what resulted, the day has been called Black Tuesday. A burglar and a policeman were slain. Forty-nine persons were wounded or injured in rioting. Nine bank robberies were committed, almost a tenth of the total number of holdups the previous year along with 17 robberies at gunpoint. Disciplined, usually peaceful citizens joined the lawless revelry and went wild, smashing some 1,000 plate glass windows in a stretch of 21 business blocks in the heart of the city, hauling away stereo units, radios, TVs and clothing. While looters stripped windows of valuable merchandise, professional burglars entered stores by doors and made off with truckloads of goods. A very well dressed man scampered down a street with a fur coat over each arm. With no police around, anarchy took over.[2]

We are an unclean lot, and as Isaiah is enveloped in the presence of divine holiness, he knows he is a sinner. Yet, this truth is not only confined to the prophet; it is true of God's people as well. Perhaps in the presence of the holy, Isaiah believes that God will now destroy him. But Isaiah underestimates the grace of God. God will send upon him, not the fire of destruction, but the fire of purification. "Then one of the seraphs flew to me with a hot coal in his hand, which he had taken with tongs from the altar. With it he touched my mouth and said, 'See, this has touched your lips; your guilt is taken away and your sin atoned for.'"

Isaiah is made holy. Holiness is necessary so that others can see the character of God in us and in his people. There are those who think quite negatively about holiness. Some believe holiness means walking all day looking as if one has been sucking on sour lemons all day. Others believe that holiness means a life of boredom. But as that great Christian thinker C.S. Lewis writes, "How little people know who think that holiness is dull. When one meets the real thing, it is irresistible."

It is holiness that brings Isaiah to the realization that these moments of worship are not about what he wants from God, but what God wants from him. Then I heard the voice of the Lord saying, "Whom shall I send? And who will go for us?" And I said, "Here am I. Send me!"

2   http://www.sermonillustrations.com/a-z/d/depravity.htm

Isaiah did not say to God, "Here I am. Send the person next to me!" No, the call that went out across the heavens was meant for him. Someone else could have taken on the responsibility, to be sure, but Isaiah realized that his service to God was not to be accepted only when it was convenient and worked into his plans. He was at the Lord's beck and call. Why pass the work on to someone else?

It can be that way among the people of God, the church today. We know that things need to be done, that there are tasks that are before us, and some, not all, embrace the "Let someone else do it" attitude. I am accountable for whether or not I answer my divine calling just as you are responsible for yours. I cannot answer your call and I cannot push mine off on you. None of us can sit idly by hoping that someone else will pick up what is still undone. I cannot wonder who are among those not doing and giving in the Lord's service. I can only scrutinize my life hoping that I am contributing to the work of God's kingdom. And only you can examine your life as well.

And contributing to God's Kingdom work in this world does not always mean that we will achieve our desired results.

Former Senator, Mark Hatfield tells of touring Calcutta with Mother Teresa and visiting the so-called "House of Dying," where sick children are cared for in their last days, and the dispensary, where the poor line up by the hundreds to receive medical attention. Watching Mother Teresa minister to these people, feeding and nursing those left by others to die, Hatfield was overwhelmed by the sheer magnitude of the suffering she and her co-workers face daily. "How can you bear the load without being crushed by it?" he asked. Mother Teresa replied, "My dear Senator, I am not called to be successful, I am called to be faithful."[3]

After Isaiah accepts God's call, the Lord prepares Isaiah for the response that he will receive from the people. The people to

---

3   http://www.sermonillustrations.com/a-z/f/faithfulness.htm

whom he will be preaching already have stubborn hearts and Isaiah's message will further push many of them away. But Isaiah must understand that his task is to be faithful, even if he is not successful in the way the world defines success. He must step out in faith and answer the call even if the results are not what he desires.

We too must step out in faith. While we hope we are successful, what is critical is not our success, but our faithfulness. It was John Wesley who said, "Do all the good you can, by all the means you can, in all the ways you can, in all the places you can, at all the times you can, to all people you can, as long as ever you can."

In other words, our response to the call of God should not be, "Let someone else do it," but, "Here I am. Send me!"

PRAYER: Lord God, in our worship this day may we so hear with our ears, that our voices will be heard as we answer the call that you have shouted throughout this world. May we be willing to step forward and to be first in line, ready to do our part for your Kingdom, that is even now being revealed; through Jesus Christ, our Lord, our Savior, and our King. Amen.

18
Hoping Beyond All Hope
(JEREMIAH 32:1-15)

In the early part of World War II, a Navy submarine accidentally sank and was stuck on the bottom of the harbor in New York City. It seemed that all was lost. There was no electricity and the oxygen was quickly running out. In one last attempt to rescue the sailors from the steel coffin, the U.S. Navy sent a ship equipped with Navy divers to the spot on the surface, directly above the wounded submarine. One of the divers went over the side of the ship to the dangerous depths in one last rescue attempt. The trapped sailors heard the metal boots of the diver land on the exterior surface, and they moved to where they thought the rescuer would be. In the darkness they tapped in Morse code, "Is... there... any... hope?"

All of us want hope. In the midst of the difficulties of life we desire hope. We cling to hope in the midst of war, in times of natural disaster, in cycles of economic tribulations. We hope; and sometimes it seems that we hope beyond hope, that is we hope beyond all that's reasonable. That is why some quit hoping, that is why others just give in to despair. Some individuals may wonder where God is in tough times, they may think that God does not care, and may even conclude that perhaps there is no God after all.

Jeremiah and his people are in the middle of what appears to be a hopeless situation. For a second time the mighty army of the Babylonian Empire has surrounded and laid siege to Jerusalem. God has already spoken through Jeremiah informing him that the Babylonians will take Jerusalem and King Zedekiah of Judah will be dethroned by Nebuchadnezzar, the King of

Babylon. For prophesying this truth, Zedekiah confines Jeremiah in the palace under guard. Apparently, Zedekiah doesn't want this bad news getting out to the public.

But even without Jeremiah's word, the people of Jerusalem know that the situation is not good. The Babylonians are much more powerful and strategically they have the upper hand. If there are those who have hope in this situation, it would seem that they have taken leave of their senses.

In the spring of that year during the siege, the Egyptians move toward Judah, and the threat they pose to the Babylonians somewhat eases the severity of the siege for a brief period of time, allowing the people of Judah to travel in limited fashion. Jeremiah's cousin, Hanamel, visits Jeremiah in custody in order to attend to family business. It is in the midst of those family matters that Jeremiah performs a powerful symbolic act of hope. He chooses to buy a piece of family property owned by his cousin.

One can imagine the initial reaction to Jeremiah's transaction. Here is Jerusalem under siege by the Babylonians, no doubt on borrowed time. Soon the enemy will take the city, confiscate the property, pillage and plunder what they choose, and take many of the able-bodied men, women, and children off into exile and forced slave labor. In this helpless and hopeless context, Jeremiah makes an investment in land about to be conquered. As Old Testament scholar B. Davie Napier puts it, in the twenty-first century this would be equivalent to the announcement of the launch of nuclear warheads and then purchasing a choice piece of real estate at ground zero. What a seemingly senseless and hopeless act.

A man approached a little league baseball game one afternoon. He asked a boy in the dugout what the score was. The boy responded, "Eighteen to nothing—we're behind."

"Wow," said the spectator, "I'll bet you're discouraged."

"Why should I be discouraged?" replied the little boy. "We haven't even gotten up to bat yet!"[1]

It appears as if that is the kind of ignorant hopefulness that Jeremiah displays in purchasing this field. Jeremiah is hoping beyond all hope. But perhaps Jeremiah's hope is founded on something that is, not beyond hope, but rather beyond human comprehension.

Judah's dire situation is her own fault. God's people have failed morally and spiritually. To be sure, not all of her suffering can be laid at the doorstep of the people, but Judah has and is about to reap what the people have sown. God has not directly sent the Babylonians, rather God has allowed his people to pursue their own selfish ways, which has opened the door to the conquest that is about to take place. The Israelites wanted things their own way and God allowed them to have what they wanted. Be careful what you ask for.

But even though God's people have abandoned God, God will not abandon them. In spite of it all, there is a future that only God can bring about, and Jeremiah's symbolic act, in which he purchases property, is a powerful statement to the people that there is indeed hope. Yes, Jerusalem will fall—pain and misery stare the people in the face; but God will restore the Israelites to their land. God has said so. Hope is not based upon wishful thinking; it is centered on the promises of God. In the present calamitous situation when there seems to be no hope for the future, Jeremiah sends a message to his people—go ahead and bet on the future. Step out in faith and trust God who has promised to deliver.

President Theodore Roosevelt said, "It is not the critic who counts, not the man who points out how the strong man stumbled or where the doer of deeds could have done better. The credit belongs to the man who is actually in the arena; whose face is marred by dust and sweat and blood; who strives

---

1   http://www.christianglobe.com/illustrationsTwo/a-z/h/hope.htm

valiantly; who errs and comes short again and again; who knows the great enthusiasms, the great devotion, and spends himself in a worthy cause; who, at the best, knows in the end the triumph of high achievement; and who, at the worst, if he fails, at least fails while daring greatly, so that his place shall never be with those cold and timid souls who know neither victory nor defeat."[2]

The people of Judah hope in the God who makes a way when there seems to be no way, by trusting in the God who will not be stopped by human convention and contrivance. It is in betting on the future that God's people prevail; for God has promised his future to us and indeed, our God travels ahead of us into the future. We should not fear the future; God is already there! It was the late Corrie Ten Boom who said, "Never be afraid to trust an unknown future to a known God."

During the Second World War, a rabbi, his wife, and their adult children were rounded up by the Nazis and taken away to one of many concentration camps. There they lived in squalor, living in very close quarters with other Jews, with no cool breeze in the hot barracks during the summer and no warmth in the winter. They survived on food rations that were not even enough for one person in a day, let alone an entire family. But in the midst of it all, every Sabbath at sundown, the rabbi lit a candle and the family said Sabbath prayers together.

As conditions in the camp grew worse, the Nazis cut the meager rations of the prisoners, and as further punishment, they forbade them candles to offer some light at night. But each Sabbath, that rabbi continued to use their one remaining candle, so that Sabbath prayers could be said. And then that last candle was gone.

A week later as darkness fell and the Sabbath approached, the rabbi took the last small piece of lard the family had, which was

2 http://www.memorable-quotes.com/theodore+roosevelt,a589.html

the last morsel of food. He took a string, and with the lard he fashioned a small candle and prepared for Sabbath prayers. His adult son was furious. He screamed at his father, "How dare you take the last little bit of food we have in order to say useless prayers!"

The rabbi, his father, looked at his boy with sorrow in his eyes, but said to him in a calm and confident voice, "Son, without food we can survive for several days. Without hope, we will not live one hour."

Jeremiah calls us, the people of God, to hope, to bet on the future, to trust that God is already ahead of us working his will. There are people who have given up hope. They have given up hope because of the economy. They have given up hope because of a dire personal situation. They have given up hope because they have tried so many times and failed, they don't want to try again. They have given up hope because even their best intentions result in disaster. They have given up hope.

Jeremiah bought a field, and in so doing he encouraged his people to have hope. How can we as the people of God in this world encourage those around us to have hope? We know that at any given time somebody will be experiencing bad times, but we also know that God is faithful, that God is with us—and so we hope.

We don't hope beyond hope. We hope because we believe in the promises of God.

PRAYER: O Christ Jesus, when all is darkness and we feel our weakness and helplessness, give us the sense of your presence, your love, and your strength. Help us to have perfect trust in your protecting love and strengthening power, so that nothing may frighten or worry us, for living close to you, we shall see your hand, your purpose, your will through all things. Amen. —St. Ignatius of Loyola (1491-1556)

19
On Speaking the Truth
(EZEKIEL 33:1-11)

Over the centuries, we human beings have had more than our fair share of characters to feel sorry for in literature and on the stage and screen, from the ancient Greek tragedies to Shakespeare's plays, from certain characters in biblical literature to the modern novel, from Broadway to Hollywood. We find ourselves engrossed in captivating story lines, drawn in by surprising twists in drama, and wondering whether the characters we have come to sympathize with will triumph in the midst of their tragedies; and when they don't, we feel sorry for them. Perhaps the most significant of history's tragic figures comes to us from the pages of the Sunday comics—yes, you guessed it—Charlie Brown.

Everyone feels sorry for poor Chuck. Life just never seems to go his way, and even his best intentions turn into disaster. Every year he is so trusting of Lucy believing that this is the year she will not pull the football away from his leg before he kicks it, and every year he lands on his back in disappointment. Every time he tries to fly a kite, there is always lurking about that kite-carnivorous tree that devours his hopes. In spite of good intentions, he can't buy even a halfway decent Christmas tree. And on Halloween night when his fellow trick-or-treaters are receiving all kinds of goodies from the neighbors, he comes home with a bag of rocks. In spite of how sorry we feel for him, we know it is true when Lucy says to him, "Of all the Charlie Browns in this world, you are the Charlie Browniest."

We have to feel sorry for the prophet Ezekiel. God has given him a thankless task and has held him responsible in fulfilling that task. Even his best intentions will be met with disdain and rejection. But God is holding him accountable for telling the truth to his people.

> *The word of the Lord came to me: "Son of Man, speak to your countrymen and say to them: 'When I bring the sword against a land, and the people of the land choose one of their men and make him their watchman, and he sees the sword coming against the land and blows the trumpet to warn the people, then if anyone hears the trumpet but does not take warning and the sword comes and takes his life, his blood will be on his own head. Since he heard the sound of the trumpet but did not take warning, his blood will be on his own head. If he had taken warning, he would have saved himself. But if the watchman sees the sword coming and does not blow the trumpet to warn the people and the sword comes and takes the life of one of them, that man will be taken away because of his sin, but I will hold the watchman accountable for his blood" (Ezekiel 33:1-6 NIV).*

"Son of Man, I have made you a watchman for the house of Israel; so hear the word I speak and give them warning from me."

Life has its harsh realities. The people of Ezekiel's day were a people whose physical and psychological world had collapsed. The news of the destruction of the capital city of Jerusalem shook their world to its foundations. The sky was indeed falling. Their central faith convictions were wavering, and along with the erosion of those convictions came the temptation to fall into doubt and despair. These are the kinds of times when it can be difficult to face the truth, when it can be difficult to speak the truth. It is so much easier in such times to utter clichés instead to cover over the pain, "Think only happy thoughts," and "Smile, Jesus loves you." It is less complicated to let the outward smile hide the grinding of teeth as one endures the harsh realities of difficult times. But Ezekiel has been given no such option. He has been called by God to speak the truth in a difficult situation and God will hold him accountable if he fails to do so. Speaking the truth can be difficult.

Henry Augustus Rowland, professor of physics at Johns Hopkins University, was once called as an expert witness at a trial. During cross-examination a lawyer demanded, "What are your qualifications as an expert witness in this case?"

The normally modest and retiring professor replied quietly, "I am the greatest living expert on the subject under discussion." Later a friend well acquainted with Rowland's disposition expressed surprise at the professor's uncharacteristic answer. Rowland answered, "Well, what did you expect me to do? I was under oath."[1]

It is difficult to speak the truth whether or not we are under oath, but Ezekiel must, for his people are in circumstances where nothing less than the truth will suffice. Ezekiel's proclamation is not going to be well received. Jerusalem's impending destruction and the soon to be exile of the people are a result of God's judgment on the people for their failure to keep the covenant. The people had already been warned, but only now that Jerusalem is on the brink do they begin to take the word of the prophet seriously.

The problem that the people face is not that of God's justice, of which they complain. God's ways are indeed just, even more than just, since the path to life is continuously held open to the rebellious. The problem is with the people's lack of righteousness; they have followed an unjust way. They have consistently chosen the path to death over the path that leads to life. It is the behavior of the people that makes God's word through Ezekiel bad news.

Nevertheless, Ezekiel also tells the truth when he informs his people that there is a remedy for the bad news. The possibility

---

1   http://www.sermonillustrations.com/a-z/h/humility.htm

of repentance is Ezekiel's answer to Israel's dilemma. In changing their ways they will not avoid the coming disaster, but they will be able to begin again and start anew even if they are in exile; and God will remain with them.

Ezekiel makes it clear that the living God takes no pleasure in the death of the wicked, but rather seeks their repentance that they may live. How human beings behave matters to God. God must exercise his justice, but even at the last hour, it is not too late to turn and be saved. The basic covenantal choice between life and death is still open to the people. The truth Ezekiel speaks is at one and the same time harsh and hopeful.

What makes it even more difficult for Ezekiel is that he is speaking the truthful word to people he must live and work with. Many of the prophets did not live with the audience of their message. Amos was from the southern kingdom of Judah. He proclaimed the word of the Lord to the northern kingdom of Israel and then beat it out of town returning home.

But even though Ezekiel lives with these people, nowhere does he soften the message for the sake of popularity; though I have no doubt that occasionally he was tempted to do so. At the time of his call, God told Ezekiel that he would carry out his ministry in "briars and thorns" and amidst "scorpions," but he should not be afraid to speak, whether the people hear his words or refuse to listen. The difficulty for Ezekiel is that he faces a community in despair so deep that it questions the very possibility for survival. "It is difficult," wrote theologian and pastor Reinhold Niebuhr, "to speak the truth to people you have come to love."

God meets the grief of his people with promises of a new beginning and abundant life. Their admission of rebellion and sin is itself the turning point, and God turns toward them with the good news that they need not perish for their severe offenses, but can instead start anew with no "criminal record" hanging over their heads. But this new possibility, this second chance at life, would not be possible unless Ezekiel, Israel's watchman, had spoken the truth.

What do we say to those whose world has caved in? What specific temptations and problems do people in such dire circumstances face? What counsel do we give those who need to hear the truth even when that word is harsh?

A pastor once made an investment in a large piece of ranch real estate which he hoped to enjoy during his years of retirement. While he was still an active pastor, he would take one day off each week to go out to his land and work. But what a job! What he had bought, he soon realized, was several acres of weeds, gopher holes, and rundown buildings. It was anything but attractive, but the pastor knew it had potential and he stuck with it.

Every week he would go to his ranch, crank up his small tractor, and plow through the weeds with a vengeance. Then he would spend time doing repairs on the buildings. He mixed cement, cut lumber, replaced broken windows, and worked on the plumbing. It was hard work, but after several months the place began to take shape. And every time the pastor put his hand to some task, he would swell with pride. He knew his labor was finally paying off.

When the project was completed, the pastor received a neighborly visit from a farmer who lived a few miles down the road. Farmer Brown took a long look at the preacher and cast a longer eye over the revitalized property. Then he nodded his approval and said, "Well, preacher, it looks like you and God really did some work here."

The pastor, wiping the sweat from his face, answered, "It's interesting you should say that, Mr. Brown. But I've got to tell you—you should have seen this place when God had it all to himself!"[2]

---

2   http://www.sermonillustrations.com/a-z/r/responsibility.htm

Friends, God's truth will not be proclaimed and worked out in this world without us. God will not do it all by himself. He has made us the watchmen over his people and has entrusted us with the incredible responsibility of speaking the truth. None of this tells us when to speak the truth and when to keep silent. None of this ignores the fact that it is not only what we say that is important, but how we say it as well. But what we do know is that the things of God in this world are too important to keep to ourselves, they are too significant to hide away. And just as in Ezekiel's day, the truth of God is a matter of eternal significance; it is the way that leads to life.

PRAYER: Lord God, give us courage to speak the truth, the wisdom to know when to remain silent, and the grace to say our words always in the context of love. Amen.

Topical Index

Scripture Index

Who's Afraid of the
Old Testament God?

by Alden Thompson

A FRESH look at the Old Testament!

$9.99

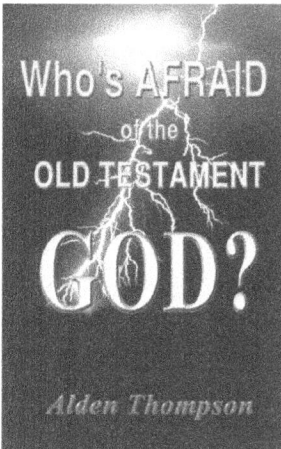

Are you hesitant to study the Old Testament? Afraid of what you'll find? Do the laws and customs seem strange and irrelevant to you?

Take a journey with Dr. Alden Thompson as he finds the grace of God in the Old Testament stories and even in some of those strange laws.

As Alden often tells classes: "You may not like the Old Testament, but Jesus did!"

Here are the chapter titles:

1. Don't let your New Testament get in the way of your Old Testament
2. Behold it was very good and then it all turned sour
3. Whatever happened to Satan in the Old Testament?
4. Strange people need strange laws
5. Could you invite a Canaanite home to lunch?
6. The worst story in the Old Testament – Judges 19-21
7. The best story in the Old Testament – the Messiah
8. What kind of prayers would you publish if you were God?

More from Energion Publications

Personal Study

The Jesus Paradigm	$17.99
When People Speak for God	$17.99
Holy Smoke, Unholy Fire	$14.99
Not Ashamed of the Gospel	$12.99
Evidence for the Bible	$16.99
Christianity and Secularism	$16.99
What's In A Version?	$12.99
Christian Archy	$9.99
The Messiah and His Kingdom to Come	$19.99 (B&W)
(an EnerPower Press title)	$49.99 (Color)

Christian Living

52 Weeks of Ordinary People – Extraordinary God	$7.99
Daily Devotions of Ordinary People – Extraordinary God	$19.99
Directed Paths	$7.99
Grief: Finding the Candle of Light	$8.99
I Want to Pray	$7.99

Bible Study for Groups

Learning and Living Scripture	$12.99
To the Hebrews: A Participatory Study Guide	$9.99
Revelation: A Participatory Study Guide	$9.99
The Gospel According to St. Luke: A Participatory Study Guide	$8.99
Identifying Your Gifts and Service: Small Group Edition	$12.99
Consider Christianity, Volume I & II Study Guides	$7.99 each

Politics

Preserving Democracy (Hardcover)	$29.99

Fiction

Tales from Jevlir: Oddballs	$7.99
(an Enzar Empire Press title)	
Megabelt	$12.99

Generous Quantity Discounts Available
Dealer Inquiries Welcome

Energion Publications

P.O. Box 841
Gonzalez, FL 32560
Website: http://energionpubs.com
Phone: (850) 525-3916

www.ingramcontent.com/pod-product-compliance
Lightning Source LLC
LaVergne TN
LVHW011207080426
835508LV00007B/653